Earn a free cert
book report co

MW00809801

The GOGI Life Tools
Mini Book

GOGI Coach Taylor
Founder/Volunteer

Getting Out by Going In
P.O. Box 88969
Los Angeles, CA, USA 90009
www.gettingoutbygoingin.org

Getting Out by Going In (GOGI) has a mission to empower members of all communities with Tools needed to build an extraordinary life. GOGI publishes its own materials. This book is intended to provide all information the reader will need to effectively learn, teach, inspire, and support studies of the GOGI Life Tools. GOGI is a non-profit organization. We develop and distribute educational materials sharing the simple GOGI Life Tools. We greatly rely on donations and volunteers to reach all populations. GOGI offers self-study courses at a discount. Donations fund these educational discounts so more individuals may learn the GOGI Life Tools. GOGI currently offers the following study formats:

1) GOGI Meetings
2) GOGI Self-Study Courses and Group Certificate Program
3) GOGI Learning Media
4) GOGI Social Media Support
5) GOGI Certified GOGI Coach Program

Note: GOGI relies on the sales of materials to help serve incarcerated and at risk individuals. Donations and the proceeds from the sales of materials are the main source of funding. Before you make copies of this material, please consider purchasing a copy of this book for yourself. Also, please consider making a donation or purchase, as this is the lifeblood of GOGI's efforts.

For more information:
www.GettingOutByGoingIn.org
Getting Out by Going In
P.O. Box 88969, Los Angeles, CA, USA 90009

The GOGI Life Tools Mini Book

This book is dedicated
to those who believe prison walls
limit internal freedom...
... and to all those who
prove them wrong.

Getting Out by Going In ~ Introduction

Getting Out by Going In (GOGI) is a non-profit organization that supports the expansion of the GOGI Community. That, however, was not how we began, nor is it the limit of our destiny.

I remember the first time a prisoner asked, "You mean to get out of prison I need to go inside for the answers?" Getting Out by Going In began as an exploration into solutions for the prisons created in our own minds.

GOGI evolved from a formal program to a community, and now living "the GOGI Way" and "GOGI 4 Life" seem to be in the daily vernacular of many individuals who were once hopeless and suffered in despair.

Now, armed with their GOGI Life Tools, these individuals find their purpose as valued members of society; no longer a deficit but, rather, a great benefit to those who witness their lasting changes. Every type of human individual is represented and accepted within the GOGI Community. GOGI is all inclusive.

Those who have found success in using the GOGI Life Tools lead GOGI Meetings, where like-minded individuals can support each other as the solution to problems that mistakenly seem too big to overcome. They are an example of service and volunteerism.

Fueling a movement to replace the old, worn prison culture might have seemed impossible, but one prisoner with the vision of GOGI expanded into two. It continued to expand to four, then fourteen, then forty, and then the explosive viral nature of GOGI took on a life of its own.

Now, it would be impossible to count the number of individuals choosing to become the solution and model their lives the GOGI Way.

This book can be trusted and relied upon as a solid support for the GOGI Culture. The heart and the soul of this book is consistent with the tens of thousands of individuals who helped form its message.

If you want training and certification options for GOGI Life Tool study beyond the contents of this book, know that published formal coursework, e-learning options, and supplementary resources are available at www.gettingoutbygoingin.org or by writing to GOGI.

Living the GOGI Way seems to be possible for all of us, and when we choose to move beyond our prisons, we find the solution that was within us all along.

With Love,

GOGI Coach Taylor
Founder/Volunteer

Table of Contents

The GOGI Life Tools

BOSS OF MY BRAIN

BELLY BREATHING

FIVE SECOND LIGHTSWITCH

~

POSITIVE THOUGHTS

POSITIVE WORDS

POSITIVE ACTIONS

~

CLAIM RESPONSIBILITY

LET GO

FOR–GIVE

~

WHAT IF

REALITY CHECK

ULTIMATE FREEDOM

Chapter 1
Getting Out by Going In
GOGI's Humble Beginning
A note from the Founder of GOGI

GOGI Coach Taylor

Welcome to the wonderful world of GOGI. What is GOGI, you may ask? In the early 2000's, I was asking the same question. Actually, my question arose out of a personal dilemma; a feeling of being trapped, stuck, and unable to find lasting joy. As a psychology student on a tour of a prison, I was confused by how familiar the place appeared. The prison looked like how I felt.

Motivated to investigate why this place called prison looked so familiar to my internal life experience, my volunteerism with prisoners began. I became intensely curious about this thing called "freedom" and why some of the prisoners seemed to have more of it than I felt I had experienced as a free person. Over the subsequent twenty years, tens of thousands of prisoners shared their perspective of the experience of "freedom," and they eagerly shared with me their opinions on how to get some of it.

Conversations With Prisoners

Through conversations with prisoners emerged the discussion that to "get out" of prison we must turn inward for the answers. Getting Out by Going In, or "GOGI" as it is affectionately called, was the name given to the organization by prisoners.

The words you read now are parts and pieces of tens of thousands of conversations. They are thoughts and reflections written down after large gym-filled seminars, as well as small chapel-cramped discussions. These conversations were held in hundreds of different prisons across the United States. They represent the highlights and lowlights gathered along my personal and oftentimes painful journey to the place of internal freedom that I now enjoy.

From the Heart and Soul

These words come to you from the heart and soul of the world's most harm-causing and often the most harmed individuals on our planet as they struggled to earn redemption and freedom.

Since 2002, witnessing the intense journey of the GOGI Students occupied much of my life. In a very real way, we were on this journey together. As a result of our shared journey and my willingness to listen, and most importantly my willingness to truly hear the students, I found a key. This key, which led to my internal freedom, emerged through my use of the GOGI Life Tools.

While life's circumstances and my own choices

never placed me in the custody of a government department, the prison I experienced in my daily life since an early age seemed inescapable. No one saw my prison. No one understood my prison. I was certain no one felt as I felt and, I truly believed that no one, not even I, could help.

In my life, I believed freedom was simply not to be mine. Believing I was simply born to suffer, I had all but given up, until that day of the prison tour when I saw what I was feeling played out before me in the form of razor wire, block walls, and gun-toting guards.

When I was brave enough, or maybe desperate enough, to look within myself for the answers, and when I was willing to sit with the suffering individuals among us long enough to explore the "why's" of it all, change happened. The sense of freedom slowly snuck up on me, and the doors to a life of satisfaction, joy, and contentment were opened.

GOGI is the journey of getting out of our own prisons by going inward for the answers, and I will be forever grateful to the prisoners who were brave or desperate enough to join me on the journey.

Please Excuse This Book

Please excuse this book for its redundancy. Somehow, on my own journey, I needed these concepts repeated to me a million different ways by thousands of different prisoners before they sunk in long enough to become a habit and eventually be integrated into the very fiber of my own life.

Within the first five years of volunteering to work with prisoners I caught a glimpse of what internal freedom might feel like. By then, I had logged more than 10,000 volunteer hours, read every self-help book on any book shelf, completed thousands of courses on psychology, and had asked thousands of questions of prisoners. It was in the repetition - including the reading, listening, and speaking of the same simple concepts over and over again - that I finally made freedom my reality. I have been volunteering to work with prisoners ever since because I believe in the GOGI Life Tools, and I have confidence in all those who use them.

Let me be completely honest with you. This book is not clever. The concepts are not earth shattering. In fact, you won't find anything new that has not been written or spoken a million times before. What you will find are the same old worn messages you have undoubtedly heard throughout your life. The only difference may be that the GOGI Life Tools and the message of GOGI is delivered with sincerity that comes from suffering; both mine and that of the physical prisoners who joined me in the exploration.

Remember, before you rush to judgment, I warned you multiple times that there is nothing profound about the GOGI Life Tools. The GOGI Life Tools are time-proven aids to help you in life, but they are not new. They are not secret. They are not magic. They are not a religion, nor are they a club or a cult. The GOGI Life Tools are not even special.

What Are GOGI Life Tools?

If they are not any of these things, then what are the GOGI Life Tools? Simply put, the GOGI Life Tools are easy concepts delivered in an even easier format that seems to work for a majority of individuals who give them a try. They are free, and they are for everyone.

In My Own Experience

In my own experience, I found my struggles were not relieved with complex concepts and heavy academic study. My struggles were not aided by scientific proof or well-meaning how-to books. My struggles seemed far too heavy for more heavy stuff to be added to my load. Why wasn't life easier, I wondered? I needed to feel like I had control. I wanted to be the boss of my life.

When a prisoner in one of the first volunteer groups commented that I was suggesting to him that he could be the boss of his brain, the first GOGI Life Tool was created. BOSS OF MY BRAIN and all subsequent GOGI Life Tools emerged from conversations with the incarcerated.

The concept that I could be the boss of anything empowered me to take charge of what was going on between my two ears. BOSS OF MY BRAIN was added to my personal Toolbox for change. With these words, a prisoner had synthesized ten minutes of my talking about the brain's function, the neurons, and the patterns of behavior into a Tool for freedom. He simply chopped away all the unnecessary and delivered up the perfect Tool for the job. They called it BOSS OF MY BRAIN.

GOGI and GOGI Life Tools

Let's get to your biggest concern, which is probably you and your life. Let's get started on the path of possibly providing you with a way to shorten your suffering, expedite your freedom, and support you in your quest for a life filled with satisfaction, contentment, purpose, and meaning.

In this book, you will learn about GOGI and the GOGI Life Tools. For most individuals, it is important to know all the Tools in a Toolbox. For others, just having mastery of one Tool is the winning ticket.

There is no right and no wrong way to study the GOGI Life Tools. They are simply Tools for any individual. Your skill in using one or all of the Tools is entirely yours to decide. Success will result from your level of commitment and investment.

Throughout the pages of this book, you are provided with basic answers to many questions asked by inquisitive minds. Hopefully as you read, the information provided will resolve questions you may have or questions that emerge.

If some of the information in this book does not apply to you, please muscle forward through the material until that morsel of wisdom or encouragement you desire makes itself known.

Please know you are appreciated for investing your time in these words. My hope is that the value of your time and money exceeds your greatest expectation and you come to realize how simple the experience of freedom can become when we choose to Get Out by Going In.

Could GOGI Be Your Solution?

There were times in my life when I've felt trapped, stuck, and locked into what seemed to be a prison for which I had no key. The hopelessness I felt about my own life reverberated into my daily choices, which further embedded me into a life over which I felt I had no control.

As I have previously shared, as a psychology student on a tour of a prison, I was struck by how familiar the prison yard looked. In an odd and somewhat indescribable way, there was a sense of familiarity in the drab buildings, impenetrable walls, and guards with guns. The prison looked like how I felt inside. I, too, felt as if my life was a prison from which there was no escape. On that day, I became committed to the exploration of freedom. What was freedom? How did it feel? And, most importantly, how could I get some of it?

For the answers, I turned towards those wearing prison uniforms, as no one on the "outside" seemed to provide an acceptable answer for the sense of despair, worthlessness, and hopelessness I experienced in my everyday life.

Tiny Doses of Freedom

More than twenty years later, I am relieved to

share with you that along the journey as a volunteer working with prisoners, my freedom was gained in sometimes imperceivable increments. It almost seemed as if tiny doses of freedom were released into my life experience through my deliberate choices, each decision adding to the ocean of possibilities which became the life I now enjoy.

This freedom I created in my life was not immediate, nor was it because someone other than me gave me permission to be free. Rather, I got out of my prison by going inward for the answers.

The prisoners taught me that my freedom was mine to plant, nurture, and grow within. In doing so, over much time, I experienced an uncommon level of internal freedom that could not be negatively impacted by circumstance or situation. The internal freedom available to me could not and would not be contained, but only if I remained deliberate and dedicated to my quest for freedom.

In my heart, I feel it is now time for the journey of Getting Out by Going In to be shared with society. Why now? Of this I am certain, many prisoners seem to be more free than those who live outside of a physical prison.

The Message

The message of this book is that you are fully capable of creating internal freedom for yourself. This message is offered as a gift from tens of thousands of prisoners who helped create, develop, and now share the GOGI Life Tools. These GOGI Life Tools are now available to you as a gift from those with prison walls of regret, remorse, addiction, gangs, and criminal lifestyles that were seemingly impossible to reconcile.

Know that prisons come in all forms and are not only for those who break the rules. Sometimes, internal prisons are more difficult to perceive as anything less than a life sentence.

This book shares the knowledge from the journey of Students of GOGI and is intended for all people, even for "free" people. It is a gift from prisoners who helped create this information I can now offer. The hope of all Students of GOGI is that physically "free" people find internal freedom without the painful journey that defined their own lives behind bars.

The GOGI Life Tools shared in this book have been created by some of the most harmful and the most harmed people in our society. If these GOGI Life Tools helped many of them evolve into providing solutions for their communities, wouldn't it stand to reason these GOGI Life Tools may help you, too?

How Can This Book Help You?

This book can help you if you:

- **Have tried.** If you have tried other methods for change but none of them seem to last, this book might provide a lasting nudge in the right direction.

- **Are tired.** If you are tired of trying, you simply want change, and you are willing to do just about anything to get a different outcome, this book might give you a solid route.

- **Are motivated.** If you are motivated for change but have not yet found that "spark" of excitement in the same old methods, this book might light that fire.

- **Are curious.** If you enjoy expanding your knowledge about all sorts of things, you may find this book intriguing.

- **Are helpful.** If you are helpful to others on the journey of change, it is likely you will find the information in this book supportive of your efforts.

- **Are in any other state of flux.** If you are in between where you were and where you want to be, then this book may help you create more distance from the unwanted.

Here's What You Will Find

In this book, you will be introduced to Getting Out by Going In (GOGI), as well as how it has evolved as a lifestyle. You will have the ability to learn about the GOGI Life Tool Calendar, GOGI Meetings, and the specifics of the four Sets of Tools as well as instructions to use each of the Tools.

The goal of this book is to provide you with Tools you can use to increase your positive decision-making and maximize your life experience. With a little luck, you will feel inspired to share what you learn with others. This is what we call living the GOGI Way.

Chapter 2
What Are the
GOGI Life Tools?

The more you read about and study the GOGI Life Tools, the more you may find them helpful in every decision you make from this day forward. For this reason, information about the GOGI Life Tools is repeated in many different ways, just to make sure you have maximum opportunity to put them to good use. The question you can ask yourself is, how might I make more positive decisions in my life?

What Are GOGI Life Tools?

The GOGI Life Tools are based on common and well-known psychological and behavioral techniques. There is nothing new about the Tools, but somehow the simple description of the Tools makes them easier to remember and apply.

Simplifying otherwise complex strategies has been the most important aspect of GOGI's positive decision-making tools. It is the foundation of GOGI's incredible success in providing anyone who is interested with a viable option for lasting change.

GOGI Is Keeping It Simple

Simplicity is sometimes the most overlooked value in our society. Individuals and societies make the mistake of thinking lasting change needs to be complex, scientific, and rigorously proven. GOGI, however, is successful because the Tools are based on nothing more than the fact that they are simple and they work. If that is a bit too simple, then the growing number of success stories may sway the naysayer's mind. We keep it simple and let practice over time prove the value of living "the GOGI Way."

GOGI Is a Simple Resource

Those of us who study the GOGI Life Tools know the lasting power of any change is dependent upon the individual's ability and commitment to utilizing every possible resource to support that change. The GOGI Life Tools just happen to be simple and easy-to-apply.

While often understated, simple is sometimes the most powerful choice you can make. Yes, the GOGI Life Tools are simple by design. Change can be simple, too, when you increase your ability to make positive decisions. You can do this through your use of the GOGI Life Tools.

If more people would appreciate living a simple life, using simple Tools, and keeping their mind uncluttered, our prisons and jails, as well as our pharmacies and doctor's offices, would have "vacancy" signs.

The GOGI Life Tools

What are the GOGI Life Tools?

The GOGI Life Tools are simple decision-making strategies anyone can use to help them create the positive life they desire. The Tools are listed below:

BOSS OF MY BRAIN

BELLY BREATHING

FIVE SECOND LIGHTSWITCH

~

POSITIVE THOUGHTS

POSITIVE WORDS

POSITIVE ACTIONS

~

CLAIM RESPONSIBILITY

LET GO

FOR-GIVE

~

WHAT IF

REALITY CHECK

ULTIMATE FREEDOM

Why GOGI Life Tools?

The GOGI Life Tools provide an easy way for any individual to get (or remain) on course for creating an optimal life. The GOGI Life Tools were developed through incorporating effective and proven psychological strategies for behavioral change into simplified methodology. These modalities for change were fused with human excellence practices gleaned from science, religions, and cultures from across the globe.

What Are the "Sets" of Tools?

The GOGI Life Tools are divided into four sets of Tools. This makes them easy to remember, as each set has a specific function. The four sets are:

　　　　1) Tools of the Body

　　　　2) Tools of Choice

　　　　3) Tools of Moving Forward

　　　　4) Tools of Creation

Tools of the Body

BOSS OF MY BRAIN is part of the set of Tools called Tools of the Body. This was the first Tool created by Students of GOGI as they explored ways to make certain they remained on track with the kind of life they wanted. By identifying the Smart Part, the Emotional Part, and the Old Habit Part of the brain, you can simplify the process of controlling how your brain operates. When you use this Tool frequently enough, you will begin to experience the power that comes with practice. BOSS OF MY BRAIN solves the problem of not being taught by example or by education that you and only you are the owner of the business of your brain. No one else is living your exact life, and with BOSS OF MY BRAIN, you can run the business of your life just like a good boss runs a good company.

BELLY BREATHING is part of the set of Tools called Tools of the Body and was created when a group of Students of GOGI tried to explain to a young student how to get out of the loop of automatic thinking. In a Circle Group, the Students of GOGI asked the youngster to lay on the ground and look up at the ceiling until his belly began to move with every breath.

This is a simple trick you can try every night when you lay down to sleep. Just lay on your back until your belly starts to move. You don't need to even think about breathing with your belly moving because it will happen on its own.

When your belly begins to move, you are BELLY BREATHING. When you notice you are using your Tool BELLY BREATHING while lying down, you can focus on doing it even when you are standing.

FIVE SECOND LIGHTSWITCH is part of the set of Tools called Tools of the Body and was created when a group of Students of GOGI wanted to find a way to get their actions to not be so reactive or automatic.

Wanting to find a simple way to stop decisions and

choices that were lightning fast and seemed out of control, they created the ability to Flip The Switch. This Tool has you to redirect any thought to a positive action within five seconds. When you have a positive action already chosen, it is easier to Flip that FIVE SECOND LIGHTSWITCH and make sure you don't make the same mistakes from the past. Flip The Switch to shine a positive light and go that direction with confidence.

Tools of Choice

POSITIVE THOUGHTS is part of the set of Tools called Tools of Choice and was created when a group of GOGI Girls were in a small jail housing module. They had very little ability to get away from each other for much needed alone time. Being in a situation where alone time was not possible, they created this Tool to build their ability to withstand all sorts of peer pressure, bad attitudes, general negativity, and drug or alcohol addiction. Being in a very difficult situation, they decided that rather than to give up and give in, they would become even more committed to living positive lives.

You can do this, too, with POSITIVE THOUGHTS. When negativity creeps into your head, you can banish it forever with your Tool POSITIVE THOUGHTS.

POSITIVE WORDS is part of the set of Tools called Tools of Choice and was created by Students of GOGI when they realized it was not enough to simply use POSITIVE THOUGHTS. They quickly realized if their thoughts remained in their head, they were vulnerable to outside influence. When they used their POSITIVE WORDS, they built an additional shield of positive protection to keep from being negatively impacted by outside circumstances.

When they used POSITIVE WORDS, they were less inclined to become victims of negative circumstances. You can use your POSITIVE WORDS as your biggest weapon to fend off attackers of your peace of mind and positive life.

POSITIVE ACTIONS is part of the set of Tools called Tools of Choice. This Tool was the obvious Tool emerging from the other Tools of Choice. This is because the Students of GOGI realized it was possible to shield themselves from negative influences by using POSITIVE THOUGHTS and increase protection with POSITIVE WORDS, but when they used POSITIVE ACTIONS, they drove away people, places, and things that did not positively support what they wanted in life.

With practice, you can use POSITIVE ACTIONS to prove to yourself and others that it IS possible to change the course of your life and be happy, positive, sober/sane, and successful.

Tools of Moving Forward

CLAIM RESPONSIBILITY is part of the set of Tools called Tools of Moving Forward. This Tool is not about claiming responsibility for the past. Instead, the Tool CLAIM RESPONSIBILITY is about today and tomorrow.

When you use this Tool, you realize that how you respond and react to anyone or anything is under your direct command. No one can make you angry. It is you who gets to choose if you will let others anger you. No one can make you violent. It is you who gets to choose if you will let others bring out violence in your behavior. No one can make you drink or use drugs. It is you who gets to choose if you put yourself in a position where saying no is a challenge. When you use CLAIM RESPONSIBILITY, you move forward, toward the life that you may never have thought possible.

LET GO is part of the set of Tools called Tools of Moving Forward and was created for people who have a tendency to carry the heavy load of their past with them into the present and future. By putting negative thoughts about people, places, and things in your hand, and giving them the Hand/Squash/Toss, you will find there is more room in your head and in your heart for positive life choices.

To actually be a better person, you move forward beyond the heavy darkness intruding in your decisions today. Regret is essential, but wallowing in regret so long that it makes for other poor decisions is just not smart. Give it the Hand/Squash/Toss and commit to using LET GO so you can move forward and make more positive choices.

FOR-GIVE is part of the set of Tools called Tools of Moving Forward. In truth, this is the GOGI "safety" Tool. This Tool gives you permission to get a safe distance from harmful people, places, and things. When you feel you are under attack or in danger, you likely become selfish and uncaring. As a safety Tool, FOR-GIVE has you ask, "What do I need to do to get a safe distance from harm?" In asking that question, you put yourself in a position to be a benefit to yourself and your family, friends, and community.

When you are safe from harm, you will undoubtedly begin to give back to others. FOR you to GIVE you must be Safe From Harm. Get safe, then give back with your handy Tool FOR-GIVE.

Tools of Creation

WHAT IF is part of the set of Tools called Tools of Creation. This Tool lets you create new outcomes for yourself by eliminating you from life's victim role and putting you in charge of your decisions. You can give everything the WHAT IF all day, every day so you can see where your choices are leading you. WHAT IF you signed up for a class? WHAT IF you didn't? WHAT IF you made that phone call? WHAT IF you didn't? WHAT IF you reached out to someone in need? WHAT IF you didn't?

When you WHAT IF all your choices, you will find that most of your choices today are exactly the same as your choices yesterday. How are you expecting a different outcome with the same choices? With this Tool you can give all thoughts, words, and actions the WHAT IF and create something different from the past.

REALITY CHECK is part of the set of Tools called Tools of Creation. This Tool is your permission to be a flawed human, but does not give you permission to remain in a flawed state. Ten Steps Forward And Two Steps Back Is Still Eight Steps Ahead. Your two steps back do not mean you are a failure. What they mean, when you use REALITY CHECK, is that you acknowledge you really messed up. But, you get right back on track by making your very next decision the most positive decision possible.

With REALITY CHECK, you understand that you are not perfect, but you keep moving forward towards positive growth with your next thought, word, and action. Your mistakes do not define you, what defines you is how you get back on track once mistakes are made. REALITY CHECK lets you course-correct quickly.

ULTIMATE FREEDOM is part of the set of Tools called Tools of Creation. This Tool is the least obvious of the Tools because it is used to create a way of moving through your day and not necessarily a Tool you pull out when something breaks down. When you use your Tool ULTIMATE FREEDOM, you make decisions that help you be of service.

You do this by being positive; that is a service to others. You do this by being helpful; that is a service to others. You do this by being a safe distance from harm; that is a service to others. When you use ULTIMATE FREEDOM, you realize that you are important as a walking and talking potential solution to all problems. As a walking and talking solution, you are living a life of service. THAT is the ultimate use of the Tool ULTIMATE FREEDOM.

The GOGI Life Tools Guide

BOSS OF MY BRAIN

The Three Parts:
  Smart Part
  Emotional Part
  Old Habit Part

Which one is the boss right now?

POSITIVE THOUGHTS

The 3 P's:
  Is it Powerful?
  Is it Productive?
  Is it Positive?

With every thought, I ask the 3 P's.

BELLY BREATHING

One Hand on my Chest.
One Hand on my Belly.
Which hand is moving?

My brain works best when my belly moves with every breath.

POSITIVE WORDS

The 3 P's:
  Is it Powerful?
  Is it Productive?
  Is it Positive?

With every word, I ask the 3 P's.

FIVE SECOND LIGHTSWITCH

Old Thought → New Action

By the count of five, I **Flip My Switch** and get to my New Action.

POSITIVE ACTIONS

The 3 P's:
  Is it Powerful?
  Is it Productive?
  Is it Positive?

With every action, I ask the 3 P's.

The GOGI Life Tools Guide

CLAIM RESPONSIBILITY

Am I Proud Of This Choice?

I am responsible for all of my actions and reactions today.

WHAT IF

What If I Am Not My Past?

No to the Past =

Yes to the Future

LET GO

Hand/Squash/Toss

When bothered, I put the feeling in my Hand, Squash it, and Toss it away from me.

REALITY CHECK

Ten and Two Rule

Ten Steps Forward and Two Steps Back is still Eight Steps Ahead.

FOR–GIVE

The Safety Tool
For Me To Give I Need Distance From Harm.

For me to give, I unhook from the past, and find my internal freedom.

ULTIMATE FREEDOM

Being Free Is Up To Me.

Living a life of service sets me internally free.

GOGI Pledge of Service

The GOGI Pledge of Service, created by a Student of GOGI, reminds us that it is through service that we find our freedom. The GOGI Pledge of Service is offered at the end of all GOGI Meetings.

May our commitment (repeat)

To the study of GOGI (repeat)

Grant us the joy (repeat)

Of giving and receiving (repeat)

So our inner freedom (repeat)

May be of maximum service (repeat)

To those we love (repeat)

And infinite others (repeat)

GOGI Life Tool Calendar

How Are the Tools Studied?

Study of the GOGI Life Tools is most often coordinated with the GOGI Life Tool Calendar of Study. Of course, the Tools can be used on their own, in their sets, or in any configuration that helps sustain positive decision making and lasting changes. The calendar, however, serves to unite all communities into a global community of positive individuals.

What Is the GOGI Life Tool Calendar?

According to the calendar, each week of study begins on Monday. The first Monday of each month begins that month's study. Each week of the month is assigned a Tool to be studied during that week. You will see there are 4 Tools studied each month. When there is a 5th Monday, all of the Tools are to be reviewed.

The suggestion of a calendar was a result of a conversation I had with a man who was housed in Pelican Bay State Prison in the maximum security unit. He was housed in an area where there were no classes, no groups. When he asked me which Tool the students were studying, he told me he didn't want to study alone.

The GOGI Life Tool Calendar was created so no one will ever feel alone in their GOGI studies ever again. When you study "on calendar," you study the GOGI Life Tools in very good company.

GOGI Life Tool Calendar

January

Week 1 BOSS OF MY BRAIN

Week 2 BELLY BREATHING

Week 3 FIVE SECOND LIGHTSWITCH

Week 4 POSITIVE THOUGHTS

February

Week 1 POSITIVE WORDS

Week 2 POSITIVE ACTIONS

Week 3 CLAIM RESPONSIBILITY

Week 4 LET GO

March

Week 1 FOR-GIVE

Week 2 WHAT IF

Week 3 REALITY CHECK

Week 4 ULTIMATE FREEDOM

April

Week 1 BOSS OF MY BRAIN

Week 2 BELLY BREATHING

Week 3 FIVE SECOND LIGHTSWITCH

Week 4 POSITIVE THOUGHTS

May

Week 1 POSITIVE WORDS

Week 2 POSITIVE ACTIONS

Week 3 CLAIM RESPONSIBILITY

Week 4 LET GO

June

Week 1 FOR-GIVE

Week 2 WHAT IF

Week 3 REALITY CHECK

Week 4 ULTIMATE FREEDOM

July

Week 1 BOSS OF MY BRAIN

Week 2 BELLY BREATHING

Week 3 FIVE SECOND LIGHTSWITCH

Week 4 POSITIVE THOUGHTS

August

Week 1 POSITIVE WORDS

Week 2 POSITIVE ACTIONS

Week 3 CLAIM RESPONSIBILITY

Week 4 LET GO

September

Week 1 FOR-GIVE

Week 2 WHAT IF

Week 3 REALITY CHECK

Week 4 ULTIMATE FREEDOM

October

Week 1 BOSS OF MY BRAIN

Week 2 BELLY BREATHING

Week 3 FIVE SECOND LIGHTSWITCH

Week 4 POSITIVE THOUGHTS

November

Week 1 POSITIVE WORDS

Week 2 POSITIVE ACTIONS

Week 3 CLAIM RESPONSIBILITY

Week 4 LET GO

December

Week 1 FOR-GIVE

Week 2 WHAT IF

Week 3 REALITY CHECK

Week 4 ULTIMATE FREEDOM

You control your life experience
more than you may realize.
With your GOGI Life Tools,
you can build the confidence
needed to control your daily
decisions so they are in the
direction of your dreams.

Coach

Chapter 3
The Tools of the Body

BOSS OF MY BRAIN

BELLY BREATHING

FIVE SECOND LIGHTSWITCH

The Tools in this section are the Tools of the Body. They are designed to help you master decisions, breathing, and critical thinking. If you make a practice of using these Tools, you will find yourself making positive decisions more often.

The Tools of the Body empower you to control your human body's decision-making process. Tools of the Body let you formulate positive decisions as a result of having control over your body's reaction to challenges. The Tools in this set help you learn how much power you have over your body and its seemingly automatic operation.

The biggest challenge in applying these Tools as an adult could be that you didn't use them as a child. Your decisions of the past probably would have been different if you had learned the GOGI Life Tools. But, with BOSS OF MY BRAIN, BELLY BREATHING, and FIVE SECOND LIGHTSWITCH, you can take control of your choices at any age.

In this section, you will explore the most frequently used set of GOGI Life Tools, and, coincidentally, the first set of Tools created by the first Students of GOGI. The Tools of the Body enable the individual a level of mastery of the mind, breathing, and redirecting attention.

In my own life, these Tools helped me build a solid foundation from which all other positive decision-making Tools could be practiced. For me, the Tools of the Body placed the point of control directly in my hands. It became impossible for me to play the victim or blame anyone else for the outcomes of my decisions. Ultimately, my responses and reactions became my own creation.

BOSS OF MY BRAIN

When I learned BOSS OF MY BRAIN, I realized that sadness, depression, and anxiety could be perceived as choices just like appreciation, hope, and gratitude. I realized that my life experience was mine to create, and BOSS OF MY BRAIN was an awesome Tool to help me create a life I enjoy. That is when the use of this Tool became second nature, simply because of the relief I experienced by using the Tool regularly. I wanted more joy and less pain in my life and BOSS OF MY BRAIN helped me get closer to those goals.

BELLY BREATHING

BELLY BREATHING provides me with a powerful resource of energy and I am returned to a state of deliberate living rather than reactionary responses.

When I began to utilize BELLY BREATHING, my life opened up not only to deliberate living, but living with appreciation. Then I let challenges slide by me with little disruption to my focus on creating a positive life.

FIVE SECOND LIGHTSWITCH

Fortified with my GOGI Life Tool, FIVE SECOND LIGHTSWITCH, there is nothing that stays in my way long enough to take me off my intended outcome. At any moment, I can Flip The Switch and shine a light on any situation. This is because I am now in charge of how long I permit a thought to linger. If I am in some way unhappy, then it is only me who can choose to Flip The Switch. My brain can then neurologically move that thought to a more powerful one.

Using the Tools of the Body is a skill that can be mastered in childhood. A child who learns these Tools before the age of eight is well poised to navigate the next phase of development with the grace and ease we all wish represented our childhoods. From birth to nearly eight years of age, children are learning to master their bodies, learning to make decisions and choices that have outcomes from which they benefit or suffer. Tools of the Body empower children to realize they have significant control over their life, even while dependent upon their caregivers.

Kids Get GOGI

One of my fondest GOGI memories is of my day spent in a Compton, California middle school with other volunteer psychology students that studied

GOGI. The principal of the school permitted the GOGI volunteers to work with a small group of kids to see what they thought about the GOGI Life Tools. The teachers were instructed to send one student from each class out to meet with GOGI.

As luck would have it, we were assigned the students the teachers wanted out of their classrooms due to the disruptive nature of their personalities. That was fine by us, as we figured the GOGI Life Tools would not work fully if they did not work in the most difficult of situations.

"Hey kids!" I said over the growing volume of voices coming from the small group of boys now seated at the picnic table. "One voice and let it be mine for a minute."

The group of eight rowdy boys looked up towards me with anticipation as I stood sure-footed at the head of the table. They had gotten out of class and saw the entire playground calling to them. I knew I had about five seconds before their attention spans were stretched to the limit.

"Who knows how an A student sits in a classroom? Do any of you know how an A student sits in a classroom?" I asked.

Nearly all the kids, sat up straight and put their hands folded on the top of the table.

"So, that is how an A student sits at this school?" I asked. They nodded with big smiles on their faces.

You Are the Boss

"Right now you all are the boss of your own brain. That is so cool. Each one of you is using the Smart Part of your brain to be the boss of your own brain and be like A students. You are using BOSS OF MY BRAIN as your Tool without even knowing it. That is so, so cool. If you continue to do this good while I am here, then I want to call the principal out here and show her that each of you can act like an A student when you use BOSS OF MY BRAIN."

They smiled, and kept their A student position as if yearning for more compliments.

"Ok. Let's see how you do with the next Tool. Follow me," I said, as I walked over to the side of a school building with my little crew following in eager anticipation, as if I was handing out candy or some other reward for their inevitable accomplishment.

"BELLY BREATHING. That is our next Tool. When you use BELLY BREATHING, you are getting oxygen to your brain, which makes your decisions smarter. Without oxygen to your brain, you do not make your smartest decisions. Who here has made smart decisions?" I asked.

All the hands went up.

"And who here has made some pretty dumb decisions?"

All hands stayed up.

"Well, if you were using your Tool BELLY BREATHING, there is no way you would have made dumb decisions, because BELLY BREATHING gets oxygen to your brain. What did I say about oxygen to your brain?" I asked, hoping at least one of them was listening.

"It makes us smarter," one belted out.

"Exactly!" I replied.

Run the Fence Line

"Ok. We are going to practice the Tool BELLY BREATHING. See that fence down there?" I pointed to the fence about 50 feet away. "We are going to run to the end of the fence and back. On your mark. Get set. Go!"

The kids took off like bolts of lightning, returning back as quickly as their middle-school feet could get them there. Gathering around me like little baby chicks, they waited for my next morsel of whatever it was that was making them feel pretty good about themselves.

"Put one hand on your belly. Put your other hand on your chest. Which one is moving? Your belly? Or your chest?" I asked.

"Belly," they replied almost in unison.

"Great. Now is the time to make decisions. Your belly is moving. You are using your Tool BELLY BREATHING. That is when you want to make your decisions, when your belly is moving in and out. That is BELLY BREATHING, and that is when you make your best decisions. Tell me a good decision you can make right now?"

"I'm gunna run faster next time," one said.

"I'm gunna sit like an A student," said another.

"I won't yell at my brother," said a third.

Great Decisions

"Great decisions!" I replied. "You are all being the boss and now you are making smart decisions because you are getting oxygen to your brain. Great work."

"Let's do it again," one of the boys added.

The boys eagerly complied and ran back and forth, automatically placing one hand on their chest and the other on their belly upon return.

"Look, my belly is moving," one exclaimed.

"Mine, too," another chimed in.

I walked away. And, sure enough the little crew was hot on my heels, excited they were learning how powerful they were and how good they were at these things called the GOGI Life Tools.

"Next, we need to test your ability to flip your FIVE SECOND LIGHTSWITCH. Do you want to see if you can do this Tool, too?" Their responses were unanimous.

After listening to the Keywords of the Tool and how they can Flip The Switch and move to a positive action, we were ready. We staged three scenarios with which the boys could relate. One was mouthing off to a teacher. One was a bully on the yard. The other was not listening at home. The boys created an improvised skit for each scenario.

The Rambunctious Student

The first skit portrayed a situation with which the boys were obviously familiar. One boy played the teacher and the other played the rambunctious student. The teacher in the skit asked the boy to sit down and the boy was going to mouth off. Instead, he Flipped his Switch and made a more positive choice. It took multiple tries, but after several minutes of nervous laughter, the skit was complete and the scenario was played out to a positive outcome. The two boys in the skit received a round of applause.

Bully on the Yard

Next up was the "bully on the yard" scenario, which, thankfully, went a bit smoother and was taken a bit more seriously than the first. In this scenario, the kid who had learned the GOGI Life Tools stops another kid from causing a fight. At the end of the skit they all shook hands and agreed to be friends. Another round of applause.

Mother at Home

Finally, the mother at home skit. None of the boys wanted to play the mother so they assigned me to play that role. In this skit, the mother was late for work and asked for help from her children. The children wanted to complain, but the oldest son Flipped The Switch and chose to do a Positive Action instead. He encouraged his siblings to help their mother, who smiled as she left for work. That skit earned its fair share of applause, as well.

"You boys are excellent at these GOGI Life Tools. You know you have BOSS OF MY BRAIN. You can always use BELLY BREATHING, and, to top it off, you can Flip your FIVE SECOND LIGHTSWITCH any time you are being pushed to the edge," I said in a brief recap as our time together was coming to a close.

"We need to tell our friends!" one boy blurted out.

This was confirmation to me of the beauty in the GOGI Life Tools. Once learned, I have yet to meet a single person who wants to keep the Tools to themself. People, even little middle schoolers, want to share their GOGI Life Tools.

Take It to the Classrooms

After a brief recap, it didn't take too long to seek out and gain permission from the principal to bring the boys into one of the classrooms to have them report on their experience with GOGI.

GOGI Life Tools

Other than the occasional nudge in the right direction, I let the boys share their Tools with their peers. The kids laughed. The teacher laughed and I marveled at how these little outcasts and perceived problem children could be so driven to share their Tools with their peers.

I asked the classroom of kids how many of them believed they were their own boss and they all raised their hands. I congratulated the GOGI boys and encouraged all students to remember they are always the boss.

End of Our Day in Compton

With that, my day at the Compton Middle School ended. There would not likely be a miracle that created "A" students out of a 2-hour GOGI workshop, but there was a spark.

Change, lasting change, takes practice, positive reinforcement, and repetition. What was obvious in the young students was the hunger for simple, Positive Decision-Making Tools among those once perceived to be the most difficult.

Tools of the Body

Tools of the Body are ideal for the eight-year-old in all of us; that part of us that often fails to remember our power, our innate right, and our responsibility to direct our lives to our greatest satisfaction.

You are not limited by your past.
You are only limited by how
much power you give it.

Coach

Chapter 4
BOSS OF MY BRAIN

BOSS OF MY BRAIN is part of the set of Tools called Tools of the Body. This was the first Tool created by Students of GOGI as they explored ways to make certain they remained on track with the kind of life they wanted. By identifying the Smart Part, the Emotional Part, and the Old Habit Part, you can simplify the process of controlling how your brain operates.

When you use this Tool frequently enough, you will begin to experience the power that comes with practice. BOSS OF MY BRAIN solves the problem of not being taught by example or education that you and only you are the owner of the business in your brain. No one else is living your exact life. With BOSS OF MY BRAIN you can run the business of your life similar to how a good boss runs a good company.

The truth of the matter is you are the boss of everything that goes on in your mind and with this

Tool you are provided the ability to understand how simple mastery can be.

With BOSS OF MY BRAIN, we break down the complex function of the brain into very simplistic components. To use BOSS OF MY BRAIN, you need to understand the three parts of the brain. The Smart Part of your brain is behind your forehead. You have the Emotional Part at the very center of your brain. You have an Old Habit Part at the very back of the brain, where your neck and head meet.

We often let our Emotional Part and Old Habit Part dictate our lives. We get emotional and react in an old habit manner. Sometimes we fail to use the Smart Part of our brain to make sense of our emotions and old habits.

When we focus on the Smart Part of our brain, we realize that the power we gave up in the past is power we can take back today. Using the Tool BOSS OF MY BRAIN allows you to decide which part of your brain you want to have the control, the Smart Part, Emotional Part, or the Old Habit Part. After all, you are the boss.

You only have three parts of your brain that need your management, and the Tool BOSS OF MY BRAIN gives you control over all three. You can think intelligently, think emotionally, or think from a series of old habits. You are the boss, even if you have not been a good boss in the past, you can be a good boss now. No one is the boss over your brain but you. If you want to manage your mind more effectively, then

BOSS OF MY BRAIN is the Tool you can use.

The truth is, you have a brain that is yours and yours alone. It is exclusively your brain and operates under your instruction or lack thereof. No one can control your brain unless you give them permission or leave your brain so unattended or drug-impaired that others can walk right into your thought process and fill your brain with garbage. Still, even if you give your brain over to someone or something else, it is your brain. You have a brain and you are the boss, even if you choose to be a lazy boss.

A Good Boss Is Attentive

In any business, being a good boss means you are attentive, you want top performance, and you know how to care for the company's goals and objectives. When you use your GOGI Life Tool and claim your ownership by using BOSS OF MY BRAIN, you are declaring that no one, no situation, and no circumstance has control over your ability to control your brain. You can be told to stand in a line, but you can't be told what to think while standing there. You and only you are the boss of every thought you create.

That being said, to be the best boss, we simplified the process with the use of the GOGI Life Tool BOSS OF MY BRAIN. We have found that individuals who often suffer from depression, sadness, hopelessness, even rage and anger appreciate this GOGI Life Tool.

This is because in some instances, for the very first time, they realize they are in control no matter how out of control their brain seems. This Tool gives you enough power to grab control of your thinking and create a new possibility.

No matter how fried or fermented you believe your brain may be, there are always new, fresh, clean, and ready brain cells being created inside your brain waiting for your instructions. It is never too late to use BOSS OF MY BRAIN to take control of your life.

If you knew, truly knew, you were the boss of your own brain, how different might your decisions be? You ARE the boss of all that goes on in your mind, for better or worse. No one but you can run the company called YOU!

BOSS OF MY BRAIN

The 3 Parts
Smart Part
Emotional Part
Old Habit Part
Which part is the boss right now?

To effectively use BOSS OF MY BRAIN, remember:

There are **Three Parts** of your brain:

- The **Smart Part** is in the front.
- The **Emotional Part** is in the middle.
- The **Old Habit Part** is in the back.

To use BOSS OF MY BRAIN, ask yourself, "Which part of my brain is in charge right now?" When you ask yourself this question, you are using BOSS OF MY BRAIN.

If you do nothing more, if you read no further, if you learn nothing more than this Tool, your life can change for the better. You ARE the boss. No one can make you mad or make you act any certain way. YOU can choose to let something make you mad, but no one can do that for you. No one can control your brain unless you give them permission to be boss over your brain.

 *~ GOGI Coach Taylor*

The GOGI Life Tools

BOSS OF MY BRAIN ✓

BELLY BREATHING

FIVE SECOND LIGHTSWITCH

POSITIVE THOUGHTS

POSITIVE WORDS

POSITIVE ACTIONS

CLAIM RESPONSIBILITY

LET GO

FOR-GIVE

WHAT IF

REALITY CHECK

ULTIMATE FREEDOM

Chapter 5
BELLY BREATHING

BELLY BREATHING is part of the set of Tools called Tools of the Body. To use BELLY BREATHING, simply put one hand on your chest and one hand on your belly. Notice which one moves the most? If you are BELLY BREATHING, your belly will move as you inhale and exhale.

Your body is designed so oxygen is transported through your blood to every part of your body. If you observe people, you will notice that many people breathe with shallow breath. You will see their chest move up and down. You likely won't see their belly moving in and out with every breath.

BELLY BREATHING is a Tool you can use to return to your optimal breath. Even if a majority of other individuals don't breathe properly, that does not make it right. Most people forgot how to breathe early in their lives and consequently are quick to anger, not as smart with decisions as they could be, and are less healthy than they could be if they practiced the GOGI Life Tool BELLY BREATHING.

Here is an interesting fact: It is nearly impossible to be in rage or out of control with anger and use the GOGI Life Tool BELLY BREATHING at the same time. If you want to learn to be peaceful inside and react to stressful situations in a calm manner, BELLY BREATHING may be a powerful Tool for you.

If you were to watch a baby breathe, it would seem as if their entire body was involved in the breathing process. In truth, that is how we humans are designed to breathe, with our entire bodies. When we are breathing in a relaxed manner, our entire body is benefiting from oxygen getting to every bit of our bloodstream.

The problem is, quite early on, we unlearn our breathing. If you walk down any sidewalk or isle of a grocery store, you will see that many individuals have their hands balled up almost into fists. And, if you watch their breathing, you will not see their stomach area moving in and out. Rather, you will see their chest move when they breathe. These individuals are not optimally getting oxygen into their bodies.

No More Fight or Flight

When we do not get oxygen into our bodies, we are often in, or getting into, a "fight or flight" way of thinking. We often anger more quickly, are short tempered, don't think clearly, and are reactionary.

Breathing with the entire body is one of the most

powerful ways to calm the body and the mind. It is the finest way to diffuse a fight as well as rationally control thoughts of anger or rage. Use of BELLY BREATHING as a GOGI Life Tool is a powerful sign of self-control, self-awareness, and maturity.

The Students of GOGI who tend to rely greatly on BELLY BREATHING as their "go to" Tool are often those who claim to be reactionary, defensive, argumentative, opinionated, or stubborn. They report that the GOGI Life Tool BELLY BREATHING has kept them from flying off the handle, overreacting, or making a mistake they would regret later.

BELLY BREATHING is designed to get you into the habit of breathing like your body was meant to breathe. Remember, it is never too late for change. You still have a lot of breathing left to do.

Breathe Like the Shaolin

One of the most famous Temples in China is the Shaolin Monastery, where Monks train in the art of breathing. Through mastery of the breath they learn to endure and ultimately conquer internal as well as external enemies. The Shaolin Monks understand that without control of the breath, there is little control over anything else.

Using your BELLY BREATHING Tool, you can endure and eventually conquer the inevitable challenges in your life. You can be like the Shaolin when you master BELLY BREATHING.

BELLY BREATHING

One Hand On My Chest
One Hand On My Belly
Which hand is moving?

To use BELLY BREATHING to break old habits and move powerfully into a positive future:

- **Put One Hand on your Chest.**
- **Put One Hand on your Belly.**
- **Which hand is moving?**

If the hand on your chest is moving, you are not using the Tool BELLY BREATHING. You are chest breathing if only your chest moves, which is the least effective and most destructive form of breathing. If the hand on your belly is moving in and out with every breath, you are BELLY BREATHING.

If this is not easy for you, try this approach: Place your feet firmly on the ground. Now, focus on your feet. Imagine that as you breathe your job is to get the air all the way to your feet.

While BELLY BREATHING sounds simple, nothing is more powerful than taking charge of how your body uses its oxygen. There is strength in simplicity.

~ GOGI Coach Taylor

Chapter 6
FIVE SECOND LIGHTSWITCH

FIVE SECOND LIGHTSWITCH is part of the set of Tools called Tools of the Body and was created when a group of Students of GOGI wanted to find a way to get their actions to be less reactive and automatic. Wanting to find a way to stop decisions that were lightning fast and seemed out of control, they created the concept to Flip The Switch and redirect any thought to a positive action within five seconds. When you have a positive action already picked out, it is easier to Flip The Switch when a negative thought arises.

When you have your FIVE SECOND LIGHTSWITCH ready, you can make sure you don't make the same mistakes of the past. Flip The Switch and you can shine the light to where you are directing your life and go that direction with confidence.

Stopping a negative thought or stopping an urge sometimes feels impossible. FIVE SECOND

LIGHTSWITCH is a great Tool to help overcome this obstacle. FIVE SECOND LIGHTSWITCH works like this: when you get consumed with "that" thought, instead of trying to get the thought to stop, simply Flip your FIVE SECOND LIGHTSWITCH and replace that Old Thought with your New Action. FIVE SECOND LIGHTSWITCH allows you to notice the thought, but not act on it. With the GOGI Life Tool FIVE SECOND LIGHTSWITCH, you swap the Old Thought to a positive New Action within five seconds.

Count the Kids

Coach Teri is a GOGI Girl who lived in the "GOGI Campus" module at the Los Angeles County Jail. When she learned FIVE SECOND LIGHTSWITCH, she modified it to work for her. She said when a negative thought entered her mind, she realized that the old thought no longer served her. She then replaced that thought with her version of FIVE SECOND LIGHTSWITCH. She would hold up her hand and name her children and grandchildren on her fingers.

Counting her children and grandchildren was her New Action. She gets to the action of counting her children and grandchildren. This would give her five seconds to swap the unproductive thought with a positive action.

When a smoker is told, "Just don't think about smoking a cigarette," it seems as if all they can think about is a cigarette. The human mind does not work well with negatives. It seems as if our mind will go to the "do not" as quickly as if you said "go for it."

As you train your mind to create positive thoughts and actions, it may be impossible to think that you could simply stop thinking about something which consumed your thought process for so long. That is why the GOGI Life Tool FIVE SECOND LIGHTSWITCH works; it realizes that your mind has been trained to head down a particular road almost like it's on autopilot. FIVE SECOND LIGHTSWITCH permits you to consider the Old Thought and then replace that thought with a New Action that is more positive and productive.

The Key Is Yours

FIVE SECOND LIGHTSWITCH is widely considered the favorite Tool of our most impulsive Students of GOGI and those who claim that sometimes things happen before they even realize they had the thought. The key is to have your replacement action ready.

The Tool FIVE SECOND LIGHTSWITCH was named in the gym/chapel at the U.S. Federal prison at Terminal Island in California when a "program" format was offered to attempt to describe the brain's neural pathways to a group of inmates.

To illustrate that their actions were controllable, the group used the overhead lights in the chapel as an example. Discussions of turning on the lights which were desired and leaving the undesired lights turned off helped get the point across.

You can think of your brain like a series of overhead lights. You get to choose which thoughts you switch on and which ones you ignore. This Tool can help you build new neural pathways and shine the light in the direction you want to go.

The more you associate any light going on or off as Flipping The Switch, the easier it will be for you to Flip The Switch in your own mind and use your FIVE SECOND LIGHTSWITCH. Light switches go on and off all day, every day, so can your FIVE SECOND LIGHTSWITCH.

Sometimes change feels impossible, or short lived. In these instances, FIVE SECOND LIGHTSWITCH comes in handy. With this Tool, we don't focus on forever, or even tomorrow. We simply focus on this exact minute and Flip The Switch to your New Action.

FIVE SECOND LIGHTSWITCH

I Can Flip The Switch
Old Thought → New Action
By the count of 5, I Flip My Switch and get to my New Action.

FIVE SECOND LIGHTSWITCH is a popular Tool for individuals who are impulsive or quick to act without considering consequences. It's also a favorite Tool for individuals who suffer from addiction. It's a great all-around Tool for every day, too. Here's how it works:

- **NOTICE:** First, NOTICE the thought. Just notice it. You might think, "Wow, that Old Thought again?" That is OK. Just noticing the Old Thought is an accomplishment.

- **FLIP THE SWITCH:** Once you notice the Old Thought, you can Flip The Switch and get to your New Action within 5 seconds. When you get to your New Action within 5 seconds, you are driving out potential for the Old Thought to have power over you.

With FIVE SECOND LIGHTSWITCH, you can Flip The Switch and direct your life in the direction YOU want.

The GOGI Life Tools

BOSS OF MY BRAIN ✓
BELLY BREATHING ✓
FIVE SECOND LIGHTSWITCH ✓

POSITIVE THOUGHTS
POSITIVE WORDS
POSITIVE ACTIONS
CLAIM RESPONSIBILITY
LET GO
FOR-GIVE
WHAT IF
REALITY CHECK
ULTIMATE FREEDOM

Chapter 7
The Tools of Choice

POSITIVE THOUGHTS
POSITIVE WORDS
POSITIVE ACTIONS

The second set of GOGI Life Tools are designed to permit you to make positive choices in three specific areas: your thoughts, your words, and your actions. By using the Tools of Choice, your daily interactions improve almost immediately.

The Tools of Choice are about creating positive choices. With Tools of Choice, you have the opportunity to show the world who you are becoming through your new, more positive choices. These GOGI Life Tools help you redefine yourself and help you maximize the opportunities you wish to attract.

Choose Your Focus

With POSITIVE THOUGHTS, you choose to focus on the positive rather than dwell on the negative. With POSITIVE WORDS, you choose to strengthen the world around you with your choice of words. With POSITIVE ACTIONS, you choose to show the world who you are choosing to become. Choice puts you in a place of personal control and power. You get to create a positive version of how the world sees you when you apply Tools of Choice.

These Tools were added to The GOGI Toolbox when the women at the Los Angeles County Jail, who participated in the GOGI Campus program, believed improvement of their choices was an essential addition to their long-term change.

The GOGI Campus was precedent-setting for its time. Los Angeles County Sheriff's Department cleared the path for GOGI to provide programming to an exclusive housing unit that was called GOGI Campus. Female inmates were referred to as "students," and the dreary block walls were slathered with inspirational GOGI posters and art created by the more than 300 women who were admitted to the campus over a two-year period.

GOGI Girls Develop GOGI Life Tools

When GOGI Campus first opened, the GOGI Life Tools were only six in number. Those first Tools were developed by men in a Federal prison where I had volunteered. The women in GOGI Campus, a pre-sentencing jail, had a far more intense environment.

A full seven days a week, from before dawn to long after dusk, the GOGI Girls would sit in Circle Groups in the dayroom of their module, creating GOGI classes based on the GOGI Life Tools and subjects of importance to them. From this daily dive into the depths of newly discovered competencies came six more Tools that completed the GOGI Toolbox.

The Tools of Choice were a gift offered by the women of GOGI Campus, just like the first six Tools were a gift offered by the men. One woman put it this way, "Coach Taylor, we are 24 women in this tiny, smelly, dimly-lit dungeon. We need these Tools added to our GOGI Toolbox or we will go insane."

Undecided Futures

The pre-sentencing stage of incarceration is particularly stressful, due to the uncertainty. For example, if a mother were to be sentenced to four years in prison and she did not have a suitable family member to care for the children, it was likely she would lose her children to adoption. The state would provide foster care, but within two years, they begin to look for a suitable long-term home for the children displaced by their parent's actions.

For one young girl, her gangster boyfriend pulled out a gun from beneath his car seat and killed a rival gang member. This meant a prison number for the girl as his willing accomplice to the murder.

For another GOGI Girl, the terror came with the agonizing realization of her drug-induced actions while running the streets. In the GOGI Campus she detoxed from heroin, and her nightly tremors and wailing were heard through the thick block walls, impacting the entire Campus.

As she cleared from the haze of addiction, she began having nightmares of selling her own child for sex in exchange for drugs. Her wailing became inconsolable as she realized her nightmare had actually been a reality.

Girls were released from jail and new girls joined the campus, each crying big tears over the events that got them there. Each contributed in their own unique way to the development of the GOGI Culture, which now offers a solution to problems and direct routes to new possibilities for everyone.

Within the walls of the jail module called GOGI Campus, there were 300 stories, 300 broken hearts, and 300 women determined to not give up. Day after day, 24 GOGI Girls emerged from their cells, stated the GOGI Pledge of Service, then sat in their dayroom seats and studied, developed, practiced, discussed, and lived "the GOGI Way."

The Birthplace of the 3 P's

GOGI Campus was the birthplace of the Tools of Choice and the 3 P's within POSITIVE THOUGHTS, POSITIVE WORDS, and POSITIVE ACTIONS. The women discovered when they filtered everything through the 3 P's, they made better choices. Before a thought, word, or action, they considered:

Is it Powerful? Is it Productive? Is it Positive?

Keeping Drama to a Minimum

The Tools of Choice helped reduce the inherent angst of jail life and permitted the GOGI Girls the ability to form the habit of using these GOGI Life Tools daily. But, while the women of GOGI Campus were actively engaging in developing the lifestyle that would become "the GOGI Way," they were not alone.

At the Central Training Facility (CTF) of the California Department of Corrections and Rehabilitation, under the direction of Warden Marion Spearman, GOGI was permitted to have more than 100 male prisoners assemble in a large gym every Friday night.

These 100 Students of GOGI would gather in Circle Groups of 8-12 group members. They would study their GOGI Life Tools according to the GOGI Life Tool Calendar in a series of 15 meetings before completing a round of study.

POSITIVE WORDS was the Tool being discussed on a particular day when I was present as a special guest. After a general meeting where I was asked to address the entire group, I was able to sit with a few Circle Groups during the discussions.

When I got to Coach Johnny's group, they were engrossed in an activity that captivated my attention. One group member stood in the center of the circle. Then, one by one, each of the group members looked their peer in the eye and stated one profoundly positive thing about them. They stated something they had observed or come to understand about each other over the course of their weeks together.

Strong Men Strengthen Others

It was an incredible sight to see as grown men expressed respect for the deep relationships created within the Circle Group. As they stood in the center of the circle, men were acknowledged for their level of integrity, insight, care for others, and willingness to become a solution rather than a burden to society.

I watched as a tear found its way down one man's cheek before he revealed through his broken voice that he could not remember hearing anything positive about himself – ever. I fought back my own tears as each man expressed gently chosen POSITIVE WORDS, which were formed from their POSITIVE THOUGHTS, and delivered in a setting of POSITIVE ACTIONS.

At that moment, while seated in Coach Johnny's Circle Group, I realized that GOGI and living "the GOGI Way" was much bigger than just my willingness to listen to an unheard population. GOGI was actually enabling these men to cut directly to the core of the human purpose of finding freedom through living a life of service. This enabled them to bypass all politics and cultural limitations inherent in the setting of prison life.

A United Force for Good

The men of CTF and the women of GOGI Campus at a county jail were on the same journey; they were identifying simple ways to reduce the angst of poor decisions. In doing so, they replaced them with a positive culture they could call their own.

What the women offered as an essential addition to the GOGI Toolbox ultimately freed the men from the confines of cultural limitations and negative norms. Through POSITIVE THOUGHTS, POSITIVE WORDS, and POSITIVE ACTIONS these men could show up in their own communities as a solution rather than a problem.

While separated by block walls and many miles, these two groups of individuals were united in their dedication, and GOGI provided a solid way in which they could collaborate on creating a solution for all mankind.

It may be difficult to believe, but there is far more positive in the world than negative. There are far more positive people than negative. And, there are far more positive experiences than negative. Your opportunity with the GOGI Life Tools is to direct your decisions toward the positive. In doing so, you will find yourself in an environment of increased positivity.

The GOGI Life Tools

BOSS OF MY BRAIN ✓
BELLY BREATHING ✓
FIVE SECOND LIGHTSWITCH ✓

POSITIVE THOUGHTS

POSITIVE WORDS

POSITIVE ACTIONS

CLAIM RESPONSIBILITY

LET GO

FOR-GIVE

WHAT IF

REALITY CHECK

ULTIMATE FREEDOM

Chapter 8
POSITIVE THOUGHTS

POSITIVE THOUGHTS is part of the set of Tools called Tools of Choice and was created when a group of GOGI Girls were in a small housing module day in and day out with very little ability to get away from each other for much needed alone time. Where alone time was not possible, this Tool was created to build their ability to withstand all sorts of peer pressure, bad attitudes, general negativity, and drug or alcohol addiction. They decided that rather than giving up and giving in, they would become more committed to living positive lives. You can do this, too, with POSITIVE THOUGHTS. When negativity creeps into your head, you can banish it forever with your Tool called POSITIVE THOUGHTS.

Only you can choose your thoughts. No one else can tell you what to think. You can choose to think of something positive or negative. It's not possible for someone to force you to think a certain way.

You Have Choices

At any moment, you can think of a mountain, think of a song, think of a television show. Try it. Change your thoughts. Your thoughts are yours to pick, regardless of what is going on around you. You can pick any thought at any time.

Here's another fact, your thoughts are more powerful than you may realize. When you think of positive things, then you will see other things in your world that are positive. When you see the world more positively, you will tend to experience the more positive version of the world as well. With this Tool, you will begin to "see" more positive around you.

Turn It Around

If you sometimes feel depressed, hopeless, or irritable, POSITIVE THOUGHTS can quickly turn things around. This is because POSITIVE THOUGHTS is a great Tool to use to turn the tide on your thinking, which often times turns the tide of events in your life.

The challenge for some people in altering their perspective is that when they are being negative, they claim they are simply being realistic. They are so stuck on being "right," or "honest," or dealing "truthfully" with "reality," that they are seeing only the negative and are stuck on how "right" they are. This poses a problem for them because they wallow in negativity, committed to their "rightness." This locks them into the negative and they become part of the problem, not part of the solution.

"Right" Is a Perspective

Until that person is willing or able to consider that their version of "right" is just a perspective held by their opinionated observation, there is little room for change. POSITIVE THOUGHTS is the critical Tool for negative individuals, but unfortunately, it is often positive people who use this Tool most frequently. Negative people often continue to be negative, and claim they would be positive if things were better.

For the GOGI Life Tool POSITIVE THOUGHTS to work for the negative individual, there needs to be enough room in their mind to consider that being negative is one perspective. The negative is not necessarily 100 percent reality; nor is the negative thought the sum total of the possibilities.

Not the Only Thought

When a negative thought enters our minds, that is not the only thought we can have. We can create many other thoughts and many other perspectives such as: "It has been worse." "It will get better." "Someone, somewhere on earth has it worse." "I can get through this tough time." "No one can make my mind negative," and an unlimited list of others.

POSITIVE THOUGHTS is a Tool we use because we may not always be positively supported by our environment. Environmentally-supported positive thoughts are easy, and often temporary. When we truly own our life experience, we create POSITIVE THOUGHTS, even in the most negative of environments.

POSITIVE THOUGHTS

The 3 P's

Is It Powerful?
Is It Productive?
Is It Positive?

With every thought, I ask the 3 P's.

POSITIVE THOUGHTS are yours to create. Here is how you can master the GOGI Life Tool POSITIVE THOUGHTS:

- **NOTICE** – I notice my thoughts. I created this thought.

- **CONSIDER**– Is my thought negative or positive? Is it helping me be positive?

- **CHOICE** – I have positive things I can choose to think about right now.

- **SWAP** – I replace all negative thoughts with something positive.

No one can intrude your mind, unless you give them permission. Every thought you have is only yours to choose. In truth, your thoughts are of your own creation. At any moment, you can think of something positive or negative.

~ GOGI Coach Taylor

Chapter 9
POSITIVE WORDS

POSITIVE WORDS is part of the set of Tools called Tools of Choice and was created by the GOGI Girls of GOGI Campus when they realized that it was not enough to simply use POSITIVE THOUGHTS. They quickly realized that if their thoughts remained in their head, they were vulnerable to outside influence. When they used their POSITIVE WORDS, it was almost as if they were building an additional shield of protection to keep them from being negatively impacted, regardless of the outside circumstances.

When they used POSITIVE WORDS, they were less inclined to become the victim of negative circumstances. You can use your POSITIVE WORDS as your biggest weapon to fend off attackers of your peace of mind and positive life.

If you wrote down all the words you say each day, are they mostly negative or mostly positive? Do you think others force you to choose a certain set of words? Do you make excuses for the negative words you choose?

Words contain the power to create opportunity, or obstacles. With a compliment, you can change someone's day. With a criticism, you may destroy someone's hope.

You Have Options

In addition to choosing to speak using the Tool POSITIVE WORDS, it is your option to associate with others who use this Tool. When you associate with other positively speaking individuals, you are associating with individuals who are in control of their lives. They are in a position of power, they can make the choice to focus on the positive.

Individuals who frequently complain, criticize, or talk negatively about their lives or others may find that the Tool POSITIVE WORDS will help them. This is because complaining enhances and encourages more negativity. POSITIVE WORDS, however, help you move beyond the negative.

Change Everything

For those individuals who are prone to seeing or experiencing negativity, POSITIVE WORDS is a great Tool to change just about everything.

First off, know that your word choice is more revealing about you than you might think. The words you choose and how you say them will almost always determine what happens in your work life, your home life, your love life, and your friendships. POSITIVE WORDS is your Tool to improve all those areas of your life, but they come at a price.

To use POSITIVE WORDS correctly, you will need to give up and LET GO of many of the words which you have heard, thought, and said for many years. You will need to LET GO of negative comments about the world, politics, family, friends, work, money, and everything else.

An Easy Filter

Here is an easy filter. Before you say a word, ask yourself, "Does what I am about to say create the opportunity for things to improve?" Don't fool yourself into thinking that tearing someone or something down has ever made things better. When dealing with humans, more is accomplished and less hurt is caused when the focus is on strengths.

Nothing good has ever come from ripping a person to shreds and expecting them to put themselves back in a better condition. That is the example we have learned from prison systems: a system which is prone to tear down the individual, punish them, and then expect them to be better for it.

No Better Than Your Words

If you are talking negatively about any human, then you are no better than the system you believe is so destructive. Until you can learn that lifting up is more powerful than ripping apart, you are no better than those who demean and disrespect you. Here is another tough pill to swallow; it is likely you will need to change first, while still under the oppression of the criticism and condemnation of others.

Do not waste your time waiting for them to use the Tool POSITIVE WORDS. You must first make the choice to get out of the system of negativity and destruction by committing to lift up others while lifting up yourself in the process.

Your Word List

One way to remain focused on the positive is to make a small list of words you wish you would hear, words you want to say, and words that can change difficult situations. These words might be created from something you read or something you heard. The key is to get them down on paper and then tuck that paper in your wallet, your shoe, or on your keychain.

The key is to have ready access to this list. You will find that when you have this list with you, the words on that list will be used more frequently. Pretty soon, the words on your list will become second nature and part of your daily conversation.

The key with POSITIVE WORDS is that you know which ones you like, you list them, and then review that list many times during the day. What you may find surprising is how others around you begin to use them, too. POSITIVE WORDS are contagious.

POSITIVE WORDS
The 3 P's
Is It Powerful?
Is It Productive?
Is It Positive?
With every word, I ask the 3 P's.

Here is how to use POSITIVE WORDS:
- **LISTEN** – I listen to what is being said.
- **CONSIDER** – Is my opinion positive or negative?
- **GET AWAY** – What good can possibly come out of this? (If there is no possibility of good, I get myself or my thoughts away from the situation.)
- **CHOOSE** – I have selected my POSITIVE WORDS, and I will use those words now.
- **CLAIM** – I am my POSITIVE WORDS. I state my POSITIVE WORDS out loud, in a letter, or as I am thinking.

Most people use the same words as they did yesterday. How can you expect things to be different when you are using the same words to communicate? The Tool POSITIVE WORDS changes the course of your life from accepting how things were to creating them how you want them to be.

~ GOGI Coach Taylor

The GOGI Life Tools

BOSS OF MY BRAIN ✓
BELLY BREATHING ✓
FIVE SECOND LIGHTSWITCH ✓
POSITIVE THOUGHTS ✓
POSITIVE WORDS ✓

POSITIVE ACTIONS
CLAIM RESPONSIBILITY
LET GO
FOR-GIVE
WHAT IF
REALITY CHECK
ULTIMATE FREEDOM

Chapter 10
POSITIVE ACTIONS

POSITIVE ACTIONS is part of the set of Tools called Tools of Choice. This Tool was the obvious Tool emerging from the other Tools of Choice. This is because Students of GOGI realized that it was possible to shield themselves from negativity by using POSITIVE THOUGHTS, and they could increase their protection by using POSITIVE WORDS. And, when they used POSITIVE ACTIONS, they drove away people, places, and things that did not positively support what they wanted in life.

With practice, you can use POSITIVE ACTIONS to prove to yourself and to others that it IS possible to change the course of your life and be happy, positive, sober/sane, and successful.

Using the Tool POSITIVE ACTIONS is your proof to the world that you are moving your life in a powerful and positive direction. What you choose to read, what you choose to do with your free time, and what you choose to watch are exactly that - choices. You also choose how you react to what happens around you. Your reaction to disappointments and how you handle bad news announces to the world who you are. POSITIVE ACTIONS is a Tool to help you give the most positive response to life's inevitable challenges.

POSITIVE ACTIONS is a powerful Tool that you can use to influence others in a positive way. When you choose to use the Tool POSITIVE ACTIONS, it is likely you will be making it possible for someone else to see an example of something positive.

Most individuals follow the leader; they do what they have seen done. If you make it a habit to use POSITIVE ACTIONS, you will be improving the lives of others, as well as yourself, even if you don't immediately see the outcome.

You Lead Your Life

The Tool POSITIVE ACTIONS puts you in a leadership position of your life, a respected position of an individual who possesses self-control and maturity. Using this Tool is a display of your bigger vision of life and shows that you are aware that challenges will come and you are defined by your reactions to those challenges. If you want to display the best part of you to the world, POSITIVE ACTIONS is the Tool to use.

If you are using the Tools POSITIVE THOUGHTS and POSITIVE WORDS, then POSITIVE ACTIONS will come fairly easily. You cannot use POSITIVE THOUGHTS and POSITIVE WORDS and not have

POSITIVE ACTIONS as a natural outcome.

Even if you are struggling with negative thoughts and can't seem to get beyond negative words, the Tool POSITIVE ACTIONS will empower you to overcome the negative.

Actions Are Your Proof

Your use of POSITIVE ACTIONS is your proof. When repeated over and over again, POSITIVE ACTIONS can help define the new version of who you are becoming. It is not enough to do something positive one time. It is in the repetition that change becomes lasting.

Just like a professional star athlete, you must practice until success becomes a habit, change is formed, and the new definition of you emerges through repetition.

You may not want to start school because it will take two, or four, or seven, or ten years to finish. You may think you can't do it, that your brain is fried, that you are too old or never really learned quickly. All that negativity can keep you from using your Tool POSITIVE ACTIONS.

One Day at a Time

It is far better to take one day at a time. Just practice using your Tool POSITIVE ACTIONS for one day. Just fill out the application. Just get on the list for class. Just attend church. Just go to the AA meeting. Just read that book. Just have that positive conversation. One action at a time. You create a better version of you with your actions.

When we take our head out of the clouds to bring the current moment into focus, we find that our lives are built on moment-to-moment decisions. Your use of POSITIVE ACTIONS may seem like a drop of water in an ocean, but with enough drops placed in the ocean day after day, change eventually is noticeable.

Just accept that one drop as one precious drop of freedom. Then, create another drop, and then another.

Sometimes we focus on those things we could have done better, or how we made a poor choice, or where we messed up. It is wise to reflect on mistakes, but it is not helpful to put all our attention there. When we remember all the positive actions we have taken in our life it becomes easier to use the GOGI Life Tool called POSITIVE ACTIONS.

POSITIVE ACTIONS
The 3 P's
Is It Powerful?
Is It Productive?
Is It Positive?
With every action, I ask the 3 P's.

With the Tool POSITIVE ACTIONS, you make a declaration of where you are headed. To use POSITIVE ACTIONS all you need to do is:

- **CONSIDER MY ACTION** – I consider this action. Is it positive or does it represent my old way of being?

- **PICK MY POSITIVES** – I pick my positive actions. I have three POSITIVE ACTIONS ready and waiting.

- **CHOOSE** – I am going to choose a positive action and leave the negative in the dust.

Things don't need to change in order for you to use your Tool POSITIVE ACTIONS. The use of this Tool each day adds up and creates a solid foundation for lasting change. One BIG action is cool, but the REAL change is in the small choices you make minute by minute.

~ GOGI Coach Taylor

The GOGI Life Tools

BOSS OF MY BRAIN ✓
BELLY BREATHING ✓
FIVE SECOND LIGHTSWITCH ✓
POSITIVE THOUGHTS ✓
POSITIVE WORDS ✓
POSITIVE ACTIONS ✓

CLAIM RESPONSIBILITY

LET GO

FOR-GIVE

WHAT IF

REALITY CHECK

ULTIMATE FREEDOM

Chapter 11
The Tools of Moving Forward

CLAIM RESPONSIBILITY
LET GO
FOR-GIVE

The next set of Tools is called Tools of Moving Forward. For some individuals, these Tools are the most challenging because they require self-awareness and insight. Some individuals would rather have things remain the same and complain about them because it is easier. The Tools of Moving Forward require that you be willing to move forward. They are for those who are willing to move beyond things that may be getting in the way of progress and internal happiness.

You Can Move Forward

The Tools of Moving Forward are about moving forward in your life. Tools of Moving Forward help you with moving beyond the past. The truth is, unless you are prepared to CLAIM RESPONSIBILITY, LET GO, and FOR–GIVE, lasting change may be difficult.

When you use CLAIM RESPONSIBILITY for your actions and reactions, along with LET GO for daily irritants and FOR–GIVE to get distance from harm, you create room in your head, your heart, and your soul for positive decision-making.

By the time we are thirteen years old, it is helpful if we have learned how to navigate beyond hardships, abuse, disappointments, and abandonments. Bad things seem to accumulate during this period of time, which is why the Tools of Moving Forward are so helpful. The problem is, moving beyond bad things is not a subject taught in schools. Parents are often ignorant or are actually the cause of the bad things, so looking toward them for the teaching might not be productive.

Moving Past the Past

The Tools of Moving Forward were created to deal with these inevitable life challenges. These Tools enable us to create the present and a future unencumbered by the negative aspects of all we have endured.

While most of us never learned these Tools when we most needed them in our teens, it is never too late to apply them. In doing so, the pain of our teenage years seems to melt away with little resistance.

In my observation of individuals in prison, it seems to hold true that life starts to unravel in outwardly noticeable ways as we hit our teenage years, often creating a spiral from which few emerge unscathed.

The pain we suffered earlier in our lives often begins to be revealed in our teenage decisions and is noticeable in our choice of friends and our behavior. We act out, sometimes not even truly realizing why.

We may show signs of low self esteem, insecurity, anxiety, depression, rage, or a wide variety of behaviors, permitting our caregivers to start slapping labels or medications on us.

The Tools of Moving Forward promote the dumping of as much early life baggage as possible. This permits us to move forward beyond the hurts when life requires more responsibilities.

CLAIM RESPONSIBILITY

CLAIM RESPONSIBILITY gives you the power to move beyond decisions of the past and be totally and completely focused on today's decisions which are most important. This is powerful because we often link the bad decisions of the past to the present and get stuck in the loop of harm, repeating the same bad decisions and naively hoping for a different outcome. Isolating each decision when we use this Tool helps us keep things new, fresh, and less likely to be tainted by the past.

LET GO

With the handy Tool LET GO, you can simply do a quick Hand/Squash/Toss of any emotion that stands in your way of happiness, thereby moving forward beyond the temptation to circle back to reengage with people, places, or things that have rattled your cage in the past. You won't really be physically "letting go" of anything when you use this Tool. You simply get the thought out of your way so you can move beyond its tendency to stop your progress.

FOR-GIVE

Lastly, the Tool FOR-GIVE helps you find safety from harm so you can move forward with creating an awesome life. This Tool has you ask yourself, what do you need to do in order to be safe from harm. When you use this Tool, you take note of what causes you harm or puts you in a position to create harm, and has you get away from that situation. In order to give to others and be of service, you have to be safe.

Are You Defined by Suffering?

In my own life, the Tools of Moving Forward were possibly the most difficult set of Tools to master. This is because my life suffering remained excusable for as long as I remained the victim. For as long as I could blame others for my circumstance, I did not need to use the Tool CLAIM RESPONSIBILITY for my present life experience.

For as long as I held tight to all the pain I suffered, I did not need to use the Tool LET GO to free myself from continual angst. For as long as I hovered around pain-causing people, places, and things, I could not use the safety Tool FOR-GIVE so I could not think beyond my own petty needs.

By ignoring the Tools of Moving Forward, I had every reason to complain and suffer. This was very convenient and, in fact, very comfortable. I was, as a result of my suffering, actually defined in a way that was oddly acceptable. I worked really diligently to not be the victim, but in continuing to recall all the injustices of my life, I just kept working in circles, never really moving forward.

For me, change did not occur overnight. In fact, my changes were so subtle that they went unnoticed by everyone, even me. Through my practice of the Tools each and every waking moment, I realized a few thoughts here and there were different.

Over time I got an inkling that maybe, just maybe, I could begin to ignore the injustices and not carry them with me to my grave.

Slow Growth Is Lasting

I began to CLAIM RESPONSIBILITY for what was going on in the moment, unhooking it from past events that would normally make it convenient to claim were not in my control. Then, ever so subtly, I would Hand/Squash/Toss away things that were daily irritants, using LET GO to make more space in my mind to focus on those things that were working well in my life.

The kicker was when it came to FOR-GIVE. This Tool requires us to get a safe distance from harm. For me, I needed distance from otherwise close relations whenever I felt heightened emotions or expectations of something different than what was delivered.

If my emotions were intense around someone else's words, actions, or lack thereof, I simply needed a "safe" distance from them until I could better manage my reactions and responses. Realizing it was unlikely they would change, and coming to terms with the fact that they were genetically linked to me and not likely to be absent from my life forever, I needed to get "safe" enough from the harm I was causing myself in expecting something different than what they were willing or able to deliver. FOR-GIVE helped me get the distance I needed to develop the skills to not let "them" control my life's outcome.

A Frightening Question

I came to the point where defining myself as my past was no longer relevant to the life I wanted to create. Who was I, really, if I was not my suffering? Who was I if I was not defined by my past? These are frightening questions when asked with deep intention to reveal the truth. I discovered it's far more convenient to remain a victim, yet, I was too weary to play out the next 50 years in the same manner.

Not Playing to Your Weaknesses

Certainly, the Tools of Moving Forward are not for the weak, but they are for the weary. For the individual who is simply tired of being tired, the Tools of Moving Forward are a welcome reprieve.

It takes every bit of remaining strength to make the decision to leave the baggage behind and take that step into the unknown, realizing – at long last – that even the unknown has to be better than one more round of the past.

Emotional Prisons

The personal prison I experienced in my life was an emotional prison created by my lack of coping tools to enable me to move forward. I was stuck in the loop of harm and the more I languished there, the deeper the hole got, and the more impossible it was for me to get myself out. My inability to move forward was the root cause for my mental prison.

The Students of GOGI would concur that a majority of their addiction and poor decisions as adults were a result of not being able to move beyond abuses or violations of their childhood. A full 80 percent of the women in the jail module called GOGI Campus reported sexual abuse as a child. Most witnessed violence. Nearly all stated they experienced trauma. They were unable to move beyond experiences and felt doomed to repeat cycles of poor decisions.

Moving Beyond Trauma

Girls are not the only victims of traumatic childhoods. Boys are molested, beaten, and abused far more frequently than is documented. These boys end up addicted to drugs or acting out in an effort to move beyond the trauma.

Their shame is often funneled into choices that may impede their ability to move forward. Acting on all they have available to them, poor choices are the only means with which they find solace. A prison term as an adult is a common outcome for these boys who suffer at a level of silence that few understand.

Who Am I?

Let me share with you a story, one of millions that make up the experiences of far too many children. We will call him R, but his real name is chiseled into my mind. He was the first prisoner who shared the horrors of his childhood with me as he waged a desperate attempt to reconcile his life by using GOGI Life Tools.

I never met R, except through his letters to the GOGI mailroom. When he began his study of the Tools of Moving Forward, he nearly halted and terminated any future study.

His biggest concern, his letter stated, was how he would define himself if not by his past. Who was R if he was not the young boy who was locked in the dog cage outside the rundown trailer called home? Who was R if he was not the boy sold for sexual favors by his drunkard stepfather who would sit and drink while R was being raped in the bedroom nearby? Who was R if he was not the man sentenced to a life in prison for murder?

We may find that defining ourselves by our past experiences is a logical method of figuring out what is likely to be the present and future. History is generally the best predictor of future events, unless there is a solid commitment to move beyond previous limits and create new opportunities.

When what we have experienced in the past will not work for the ever-so-faint vision of the future, that is when the Tools of Moving Forward come in handy.

Chapter 12
CLAIM RESPONSIBILITY

CLAIM RESPONSIBILITY is part of the set of Tools called Tools of Moving Forward. This Tool is not about claiming responsibility for the past. Instead, the Tool CLAIM RESPONSIBILITY is about today and tomorrow. When you use this Tool, you realize that how you respond and react to anything is under your direct command. No one can make you angry. It is you who chooses to let others anger you. No one can make you violent. It is you who chooses if you will let others bring out violence in you. No one can make you drink or use drugs. It is you who chooses if you put yourself in a position where saying no is a challenge. When you use CLAIM RESPONSIBILITY, you move forward toward a life you may have never thought possible.

There are many ways to interpret the words "claim" and "responsibility." With how GOGI uses these words, they provide a powerful way to gain perspective with which you can move forward in your life.

There were many things that happened to and around you in the past, many of them were your responsibility and many were not your responsibility, or you had no knowledge or choice in the matter. Using CLAIM RESPONSIBILITY as a GOGI Life Tool is not about the past at all.

GOGI does not focus on reconciling the past because it could take years, possibly a lifetime, to understand what occurred and unravel the mess that resulted. GOGI is about creating a positive future for individuals trying to resolve the past. The fact is, the past is more easily reconciled when you have momentum moving positively into the present and future.

Your Choices

Rather than remain stuck and unable to move forward, CLAIM RESPONSIBILITY is about your choices today. It is kind of like having a broken car at the side of the road, but not having any tools or help to fix it. You can remain at the side of the road all day long complaining about how you have a broken car, or you can gather up the things you need, shut the car door, and start walking toward your freedom.

Today Is Yours

The Students of GOGI don't want you to remain stuck in the past forever, reliving what you did or what happened. That actually creates a vacuum and disables any insight you might gain from the past. CLAIM RESPONSIBILITY as a Tool states that no matter what happened or what you did in the past, today is yours to become part of the solution and make positive decisions.

With CLAIM RESPONSIBILITY, you have power over your actions and reactions today and forevermore. It does not diminish your actions of the past or permit you to remain stuck in them. Getting unstuck is the key to developing insight.

When you use CLAIM RESPONSIBILITY, how you act and how you react is no longer tied to a terrible childhood, an addiction, a criminal background, a gang membership, not having a father/ mother, drinking too much, a greedy mentality, a death, a betrayal, abuse, or anything else which might have provoked you to do things you later regret.

Gaining Forward Momentum

If you are an individual with a lot of history and a heavy weight of the past slowing your ability to move forward, CLAIM RESPONSIBILITY permits you to gain forward momentum. Once you have forward momentum, the past is more easily reconciled, insight can be achieved, and lasting change can occur.

We use CLAIM RESPONSIBILITY in a slightly different manner than the words suggest. Remember, we are using CLAIM RESPONSIBILITY as a Tool, not as something your teacher, parent, counselor, politics, family, friends, work, money, and everything else want you to do. CLAIM RESPONSIBILITY is a proactive Tool that relates to the future.

You can certainly claim an appropriate level of responsibility for your actions of the past. That is different than using CLAIM RESPONSIBILITY as a GOGI Life Tool. This is because at GOGI, we are less concerned about the past and more concerned about your ability to make better choices today. We find that CLAIM RESPONSIBILITY promotes positive decision-making today and tomorrow.

The Tool and the Process

As a Tool, you can use CLAIM RESPONSIBILITY to take charge of your actions, your reactions, your opinions, your words, and your responses to every single thing from this day forward. Your Tool CLAIM RESPONSIBILITY does not let anyone else take over your life creating process.

With CLAIM RESPONSIBILITY, everyone and everything is kept out of the decision making boardroom of your brain. Only YOU are in charge of how you react, act, perceive, and respond. With CLAIM RESPONSIBILITY as a GOGI Life Tool, you will never say, "He made me mad;" "It's your fault;" Or, "If it was not for my situation, I would be happy." That kind of thinking is not going to help you create freedom in your life. It disables you and makes you a victim of circumstance.

At GOGI, we know you can be the creator of a better life, and CLAIM RESPONSIBILITY is your Tool to help.

CLAIM RESPONSIBILITY
Am I Proud of This Choice?
I am responsible for all of my actions and reactions today.

As a GOGI Life Tool, CLAIM RESPONSIBILITY is easy because it has less to do with the past and everything to do with this moment, on this day, and from now on. Here is how to use CLAIM RESPONSIBILITY:

- **CONSIDER** – What is happening around me?
- **I AM IN CHARGE** – I am in charge of my actions and reactions today.
- **I OWN IT** – I can choose how to respond right now. I own today.

CLAIM RESPONSIBILITY is a great way to stop blaming others, the system, or your past self for things. It puts you in control of your life from this day forward. Ask yourself, "Am I Proud of This Choice?"

How you react and how you respond is 100 percent in your control when you use CLAIM RESPONSIBILITY. With this Tool, today becomes yours to create as a positive step forward in your life.

~ GOGI Coach Taylor

The GOGI Life Tools

BOSS OF MY BRAIN ✓
BELLY BREATHING ✓
FIVE SECOND LIGHTSWITCH ✓
POSITIVE THOUGHTS ✓
POSITIVE WORDS ✓
POSITIVE ACTIONS ✓
CLAIM RESPONSIBILITY ✓

LET GO
FOR-GIVE
WHAT IF
REALITY CHECK
ULTIMATE FREEDOM

Chapter 13
LET GO

LET GO is part of the set of Tools called Tools of Moving Forward and was created for people who have a tendency to carry the heavy load of their past with them into the present and the future. By putting negative thoughts about people, places, and things in your hand and giving them the Hand/Squash/Toss, you will find there is more room in your head and in your heart for more positive life choices. To actually be a better person, you must move forward beyond the heavy darkness intruding your decisions today. Regret for harm caused is essential, but wallowing in regret for so long that it creates other poor decisions will not going to help you move forward. Give it the Hand/Squash/Toss and commit to using LET GO so you can move forward and make more positive choices.

LET GO can be a challenging Tool for many people. This is often because once something happens, something terrible or massively influential, your life changes around that event. Thoughts, words, actions, and your very being adjust to what happened.

For example, it could be that someone close to you was killed or something really bad happened to you as a child. It could be the first time you got high or when you were abandoned or betrayed. It could be the trauma you experienced from falling victim to an addiction which stole years of your life.

Whatever the negative event was, it became part of your identity, causing you to exclude choices and decisions which may have been more positive.

LET GO might sound like an easy Tool, but it is not easy for many individuals. Here's an example which shows just how difficult it can be. If you swap the situation described below to fit your own life, you will understand why the Tool LET GO seems nearly impossible for many people. Could it be that holding on to the past is the reason people play out negative and unproductive lifestyles?

Who Are You?

Let's say, in this example, you have identified yourself as someone from "Your City" all your life. You are "The One" everyone comes to for advice and counsel. Your life in "Your City" just so happens to create an environment where drugs, crime, and people getting locked up are normalized. You are important in "Your City." You have a place, a life, a reputation, and a history.

But, what happens if you move forward in your life and are not living in "Your City," and instead you move somewhere where no one knows you? What happens if you are in another town?

Here is what probably happens. Your entire identity may be changing. It's a challenge because you do not feel accepted by the people in the new town because you think, talk, and act like someone who has been around drinking, drugs, jail, and violence your entire life. It is likely you identify with the people in the new town who are similar to your past and they drink, do drugs, and talk a lot about things that are illegal. For as long as you do not LET GO, you are holding on.

So, What's Next?

Do you see that using the Tool LET GO may not always be easy? The LET GO Tool is not always easy, nor is it for the weak. Using LET GO for those things that create negativity in your life can seem lonely, boring, confusing, or depressing. In this case, the Tool LET GO may seem downright impossible to use successfully. People often ask, "If I use LET GO, then what will I get as a replacement?" If you no longer identify yourself as someone of importance in "Your City," then who are you?

Here is another example. If your focus is to do whatever it takes to be a drug treatment counselor for kids, then that new identity needs to be so clear in your mind that the old identity is replaced, and you begin to be an example for good. Having something positive to hold on to makes the use of LET GO easier.

LET GO In Present Time

Additionally, the GOGI Life Tool LET GO permits you to handle the present more powerfully. Use LET GO to rid yourself of the need for instant retaliation which will only get you in more trouble. Did someone disrespect you? Has someone lied, cheated, or stole? Use LET GO to replace the need for immediate revenge.

Use LET GO to keep from overreacting, reacting too quickly, creating drama, or dragging others down that old worn-out road which leads to trouble. The Tool LET GO keeps you from falling back into old patterns because you Hand/Squash/Toss your way into the future.

Lighten Up With LET GO

LET GO helps you move beyond all that has happened and all the negative which is included in your definition of self. LET GO is a great Tool if you are tired of carrying the weight of negativity around throughout your life. And, it will require practice.

Practice is the only way we can perfect a skill. LET GO is a Tool, but use of the Tool can become a skill. This Tool can still be painful for some which is why we keep it simple. We do not want you to try to use LET GO for the big stuff too soon.

After all, it is the big stuff which may have defined you for a very long time. It would be impractical to suggest you simply use LET GO of the very thing which consumed your life thus far.

A die-hard Student of GOGI wrote this about the Tool LET GO, "I sit here now with the last of my life story, but afraid to use LET GO because I feel maybe I will disappear."

What a profound realization he had while on his GOGI journey. When what we have experienced in our life IS our life, how CAN we use LET GO?

The Little Stuff

So, rather than feel as if you may disappear, you can use LET GO on the little stuff. Here is an example. Is someone making noises that are irritating? Rather than let it irritate you, practice LET GO. Use the Tool LET GO and rid yourself of anything which might hold you back from being or feeling your best. Is your depression causing you to swim in a sea of negativity? Use the Tool LET GO and rid yourself of thoughts which keep you in negative waters.

Students of GOGI tell us the simple act of putting the negativity in the palm of their hand, squashing it, and then tossing it away gets the emotion and the negativity out of their body so they can think more positively.

Keep It Simple

Keeping it simple is always the best way to learn a new skill. When you can put most of life's irritations in the palm of your Hand, Squash them, and Toss them out of your mind, only then will you be prepared to start tackling the big stuff.

Using the Tool LET GO could be your freedom

from being the victim or creating a victim, but it is important to use the Tool LET GO to stop victimizing yourself with negativity first. Use LET GO for the little stuff and sometimes the big stuff disappears along the way. You won't disappear, but the negativity diminishes and the new you has room to emerge.

Hand/Squash/Toss

A simple way to use LET GO, when in doubt, is to put the thought that is bothering you in your hand and give it the Hand/Squash/Toss. When you use LET GO, you are free to move forward.

People tend to remember hurts and often carry the memory far into their future. At some point, however, the weight of the past becomes a burden. This tends to hold us back from a bright future.

When we learn to LET GO with the GOGI Life Tool, we are freed from the heavy load of the past and find the freedom to move bravely into the future.

Coach

LET GO

Hand/Squash/Toss

When bothered, I put the feeling or thought in my Hand. I Squash it, and Toss it away from me.

LET GO is challenging for some, but here is a simple way to begin to practice LET GO in your daily life. Eventually, you will be able to use LET GO of the big stuff that causes big pain. Here is how to use LET GO every day:

- **HAND** – I imagine that thought or feeling in my Hand, out of my mind and out of my body.

- **SQUASH** – I crumple up that concern, thought, or feeling. I have the power to Squash it.

- **TOSS** – I can LET GO and Toss it in the trash, the toilet, the sky, or to the ground. I LET GO and let it go.

- **LET GO** – Out loud or silently I say, "I LET GO of anything and everything that holds me back."

Once you get really good at using LET GO and are ready to move beyond day-to-day irritations, you can use LET GO to help you move beyond the big stuff, too.

~ GOGI Coach Taylor

The GOGI Life Tools

BOSS OF MY BRAIN ✓
BELLY BREATHING ✓
FIVE SECOND LIGHTSWITCH ✓
POSITIVE THOUGHTS ✓
POSITIVE WORDS ✓
POSITIVE ACTIONS ✓
CLAIM RESPONSIBILITY ✓
LET GO ✓

FOR-GIVE

WHAT IF

REALITY CHECK

ULTIMATE FREEDOM

Chapter 14
FOR-GIVE

FOR-GIVE is part of the set of Tools called Tools of Moving Forward. In truth, this is the GOGI "safety" Tool. This Tool gives you permission to get a safe distance from harmful people, places, and things. When you are a safe distance from harm you will naturally find yourself giving back to others. As a safety Tool, FOR-GIVE has you asking what you need to do to get a safe distance from harm. In asking that question, you are putting yourself in a position to be a benefit to yourself, your family, your friends, and your community. When you are safe from harm, you will undoubtedly begin to give back to others. FOR you to GIVE, you must be Safe From Harm. Get safe, then give back with your handy Tool FOR-GIVE.

FOR–GIVE as a Tool is not about forgiveness. The two are different. FOR–GIVE is a Tool, not a concept. Most religions and cultures teach the power of forgiveness, which frees you from many negative emotions and feelings. The difference is that the GOGI Life Tool FOR–GIVE can help you come to a greater understanding and easier application of forgiveness in your life.

FOR–GIVE as a Tool requires that you protect yourself. This is because it is not wise to forgive someone for hitting you when they are standing in front of you with their fists raised. You would be much wiser to protect yourself first. Forgiveness is not wise when danger is at hand. If you are suffering from a Meth addiction, it is not wise, or even possible, to forgive yourself while you are actively using or just beginning the recovery process.

When you use the Tool FOR–GIVE, you need to be open to creating a new support system, a change of peers, an alignment with an alternative culture, and practice of skills and Tools to move beyond the vulnerable state in which you find yourself. FOR–GIVE is a Tool you can use to remind yourself to get distance from harm.

FOR-GIVE Is Not Forgive

A child who suffered sexual abuse can use the Tool FOR–GIVE when they are no longer at risk for continuation of the abuse, even if this can only occur when they become an adult. An individual can also use the Tool FOR–GIVE to move beyond the actions of their past if they have truly corrected their thinking and behavior so they are not in danger of repeating the same action. FOR–GIVE, as a GOGI Life Tool, states that it is not enough to say or hear the words "I am sorry." There must be safety from further harm for the Tool FOR–GIVE to work properly.

FOR–GIVE requires distance, protection, and the positive choices which lead to freedom. This does not mean you do not feel remorse or trauma for what happened, but it does mean that you do not need to relive the past over and over again.

More Than the Past

Reliving the past only creates more of the past. If you wallow in the past, your present and your future will be filled with wallowing and may result in more angst and more pain. This creates more negativity. To develop insight and lead a meaningful life, you can be of positive service to others, no matter what has happened in the past.

Using the GOGI Life Tool FOR–GIVE is as simple as asking yourself, "Am I still at risk of being hurt or hurting others?" If you are at risk, you need to protect yourself. If you are safe from harming self or others, then FOR–GIVE permits you to have a new perspective of being of service and giving back.

Get Distance

No matter what you did, or what "they" did, or what you experienced, or the harm you caused, if you don't want it to happen again, then you can use your Tool FOR–GIVE to move forward. FOR–GIVE can be thought of as a Tool to help you give back, using what happened in the past as your testament of how much any individual can change. "For Me To Give, I must be

Safe From Harm." That is the Tool FOR-GIVE.

FOR-GIVE Is an Action

Forgive is a word that is used frequently and asked of us with equal frequency. FOR–GIVE as a GOGI Life Tool, however, is very different from the word forgive. FOR–GIVE as a Tool is an action item. It requires action on your part and has little to do with engaging in conversation with another.

Don't misunderstand; At GOGI we know forgiveness is important. To address hurts and harms with others, to ask for, and to give, forgiveness is the backbone of nearly every spiritual study, religion, and culture.

At GOGI, FOR–GIVE is simply a Tool you can use to get beyond the hurt or harm caused by self or others. When you get beyond the harm, it is easier for forgiveness to emerge.

The Protection Tool

FOR–GIVE is about creating safety and protection. The real question in using the Tool FOR–GIVE is, "Are you a sufficient distance from the harm-causing person or circumstance?" With this Tool, you look for protection from further harm, because until you are a sufficient distance from the harm, there is no point in trying to forgive. As a Tool, FOR–GIVE requires you to get distance from the harm. Let's say your harm is a gambling habit. You can say, "Sorry" or, "Please forgive me" a million times, but if you don't stop gambling, you are too close to harm. Harm is still hovering.

The Tool FOR–GIVE requires that you do any and every thing to distance yourself from harmful actions and harmful people.

For You to Give

Ultimately, FOR–GIVE is your Tool FOR you to GIVE back, give to others, and get out of the limits created by the harm. When we are harmed or harm ourselves, our world begins to revolve around the harm and we lose sight of our innate need to GIVE to others. FOR us to GIVE, we must be safe enough from harm that our world gets larger and includes observing and serving the needs of others.

FOR us to GIVE, we need distance from harm. That is the critical difference between forgiveness as a spiritual concept and FOR–GIVE as a GOGI Life Tool.

For me to give back to others…
For me to help those who are hurting…
For me to be all I can be…
I MUST BE SAFE FROM HARM.

FOR-GIVE

The Safety Tool
For Me To Give, I Need Safety From Harm.
For Me To Give, I unhook from the past and find my internal freedom.

FOR–GIVE is your safety Tool. FOR-GIVE is your permission to move forward and put a stop to recurring pain. In a real way, FOR–GIVE is your ticket away from the harm, even if you were the one who caused the harm. Here is how to use the GOGI Life Tool FOR–GIVE:

- **WHAT IS THE HARM?** – What hurts the most? Where in my life do I hold resentments? Where am I disappointed, in rage, or angered?

- **GET DISTANCE** – Am I a sufficient distance from potential harm? Is there a way for me to be hurt this way again? If so, I will get away.

- **FOR the GIVE** – For Me to Give, I unhook from the past and get to safety. With my new distance from the harm, I can choose to do something nice for someone else. I choose to be of service.

Chapter 15
The Tools of Creation

WHAT IF

REALITY CHECK

ULTIMATE FREEDOM

The next set of Tools we will explore in the following chapters are the Tools of Creation. These Tools permit you to create a positive life experience, regardless of your current situation. The Tools of Creation permit you to become creative with your future. The Tools of Creation help you move powerfully into the life you have always wanted, but a life you may not have thought possible.

This set of Tools was designed to free you from the perception that things will not change or your life is limited to current circumstances. If you diligently practice the three Tools in this set, you will find unlimited and unrestricted potential for your life within your grasp.

The Tools of Creation require you to be brave enough to consider your life as more than circumstantial and consider yourself as more than a victim of situations.

You Get to Dream

With your GOGI Life Tools, you get to dream with WHAT IF and make room for new and different possibilities. REALITY CHECK lets you come to realize you are not perfect and you are likely to make mistakes. REALITY CHECK keeps shame and hopelessness out of the change process and permits you to quickly recover from your mistakes. ULTIMATE FREEDOM is about using the most positive aspects of who you are to create a better world. Living your life in service of others is the only true and lasting freedom that does not require the convenience of things going your way. ULTIMATE FREEDOM can never be taken away and it gives back much more than the investment you make.

Bravery Isn't Cheap

Bravery has a few requirements for sustainability. It requires faith in something greater or more powerful than oneself. For some, this may be reliance upon God or faith in a divine order of things. For others, it is a mission or vision for the future that is so strong that natural fear is overshadowed. For some individuals like me, bravery was the last option available. Blaming others, cursing the "system," and complaining about all I had been denied didn't seem to work very well.

Regardless of how you get to the need for bravery,

be it divine or desperation, it will take a consistent dose of bravery before the Tools in this set even begin to make sense. Be forewarned, there are multiple forms of bravery and only one form works in developing a sustainable freedom. There is the bravery that comes with adrenaline rush. This is temporary. There is the bravery that is the slow burn. This requires tending to the slow burn you keep aflame even during a torrential downpour.

Bravery is Developed Daily

The good news is, and I can personally attest to this, bravery can be developed. Like most of us, I was not born automatically brave. This was an aspect of my life that I cultivated over years of determination. I have witnessed it in others, I have done it for myself, and I speak from my heart when I say that you will experience great levels of internal freedom growing incrementally when you nurture the slow burn of bravery.

To do this, you can start small. Pick one simple action each day that requires you to expand and grow beyond your current comfort level. This may be as simple as picking a positive word of the day and making certain you use that word in conversations no fewer than ten times before you pull your feet up off the floor at nightfall. It may be as simple as making eye contact and offering a smile to a specific type of person you have previously ignored. It can be as simple as brushing your teeth with the opposite hand than you have dictated as your regular toothbrush holding hand. Doing the small things differently creates bravery for doing the bigger things differently, too. Developing long lasting bravery is best when in small and consistent doses.

Getting Your Creations Going

This set of Tools, WHAT IF, REALITY CHECK, and ULTIMATE FREEDOM, is about your often-hidden powers to direct your life's outcomes. If a specifically desired outcome is not likely, you are able to create the unrestricted experience of freedom within your physical limitations– even in the face of what appears to be an immovable obstacle.

For example, the individual who has lost an arm may use all the GOGI Life Tools in the world, but the original arm is not going to be re-attached to the body. Using the GOGI Life Tools, however, it is possible for this individual to develop the ability to emotionally empower other physically disabled individuals. It is possible to develop reading or video materials to help new amputees deal with the inherent challenges of losing a limb. It is possible for this individual to seek support for a robotic or prosthetic arm. There are opportunities to make a positive contribution even while experiencing limitations.

The point is, while some facts simply will not change, how you manage to create freedom beyond those facts defines your creative life expression. That is when your bravery comes into play. Luckily, within each set of GOGI Life Tools are the natural and simplified building blocks for bravery. This enables you to create from a place of strength and not suffer from a place of perceived victimization of oneself.

When taught to individuals who are actively and bravely engaged in the quest for freedom, the Tools of Creation seem to act in the same way an injection of NOS does to a race car, catapulting the individual to even greater levels of internal freedom.

WHAT IF

When GOGI Girl Teri rushed down the stairs from her second-tier jail cell and excitedly approached me with childlike enthusiasm, the WHAT IF Tool was added to the GOGI Toolbox.

"Coach Taylor, Coach Taylor!" she exclaimed.

"Yes, Teri. What is it?" I replied.

"Coach Taylor. What if I am not my past?"

WHAT IF was added to the GOGI Toolbox that day. Until that moment it had never occurred to me that some individuals would remain stuck in defining themselves by their past actions, but that is truly the case.

Addiction may cause an individual to define their life by a substance and as a result, they feel helpless, hopeless, and even powerless to make a change. Addiction is like other circumstances in which you may choose to define yourself or you may create other constructs that limit your freedom.

Saying, "I am a Meth addict" is a different perspective than, "I am addicted to Meth." Meth addiction does not need to be the limit of their life experience.

The question Teri asked is one we all may ask ourselves with each and every decision. WHAT IF there is another possibility just around the corner that is just as valid, just as strong, just as truthful?

Teri realized that although she was powerless over the way things were presented to her in life, she was entirely in control over the things related and her attitude towards them.

Only the brave (or in my case, totally desperate) individual is willing to question every preconceived notion. The brave, or the desperate, ask questions in an effort to break free of otherwise limiting self-definition.

Here is a real-life example. I travel often, visiting GOGI Leaders and helping them expand the GOGI Culture. While on the road, credit cards are used, suitcases are moved around, rental cars and motels are used. I am fairly vulnerable, in that my internet connections are frequently public and shared with some individuals who have not yet been exposed to the joy of living "the GOGI Way."

I have been stolen from, lied to, and manipulated as a result of the vulnerability from having a lot of public contact and exposure to strangers. For a while, I believed I had no control over thieves who tap into credit cards and bank accounts to steal money. I believed it was just part of the pain and disappointment I had to endure in making myself available to those who were limited in awareness of the joy that comes from positive life choices.

With WHAT IF, however, I came to realize that I have great power over my computer passwords and where I log onto the internet.

Ultimately, I can protect credit cards, identification cards, and other documents. In using this Tool, I realize I am not powerless over thieves, as there are specific actions I can take to reduce my vulnerability. Sure, I am powerless over thieves if I am careless, but I am no longer careless. I am no longer complacent about being violated and treated less than honorably. I am, in fact, brave when I use my WHAT IF Tool. I use my WHAT IF and I ask, "WHAT IF I avoid as much possible danger as I am able?"

I have even gotten so good at this Tool that I can now help others protect themselves as well. I quite regularly remind volunteers not to leave doors unlocked, not to leave purses or wallets or cash in plain view, not to leave anything visible in a car, not to leave bicycles outside even if they are locked, not to tempt anyone to live in a way that is inconsistent with enhancing the safety of others.

Do not tempt the weak, expecting them to be strong. As a Student of GOGI, I know I can fortify a weak situation by making strong and positive choices.

WHAT IF is about expanding beyond a limiting "reality" and defining the world from a perspective of strength. WHAT IF you are not your past? Who are you? That is what this Tool has you ask yourself.

REALITY CHECK

Before it became one of the GOGI Life Tools, there were Tools with which to make more positive decisions, but there was a void in allowing mistakes, failure, and backslides to be experienced from a place of power and learning. REALITY CHECK is the Tool used when, as we explore and expand our life experiences, we fall short of perfection and sometimes create quite a mess of things.

This tendency to make one poor decisions and give up is particularly common with individuals suffering from addiction. This scenario played itself out all too often with Students of GOGI in the formative years of the GOGI Culture.

REALITY CHECK was a Tool born of many tears and shattered hopes as GOGI Girls were released from the GOGI Campus at the Los Angeles County Jail. They tended to be certain that armed with their GOGI Life Tools they would remain sober.

Then, before we could celebrate their successes, I would receive word from jail staff that our very confident GOGI Girl was back in "Receiving" at the jail, arrested for yet another drug offense.

What I found when I interviewed these women, is that this failure came as a bigger blow than all prior arrests. They were "certain" that having the GOGI Life Tools would have guaranteed a perfect life, free from the addiction that plagued them for many years leading up to their opportunities at the GOGI Campus.

REALITY CHECK helped each one of them realize the "Ten Steps Forward" they experienced in their Campus training were not erased by the "Two Steps Back" that resulted in re-arrest. No one could take away the Ten Steps Forward and the knowledge gained in each of those steps, and only they were responsible for the Two Steps Back. REALITY CHECK was added to the GOGI Toolbox to offer a positive outcome, even amid the imperfections of human life.

ULTIMATE FREEDOM

ULTIMATE FREEDOM is a self-regeneration Tool in that the more you use it, the more it shows up in other aspects of your life. This Tool is like putting on a pair of goggles with enhanced vision capabilities that permit you to see beneath the superficial nature of daily life and into the bigger picture of all things.

When armed with ULTIMATE FREEDOM, and the perspective it enhances, you continually experience the power of purpose and meaning. This Tool is all about your ability to be a creator of positivity, and to bless the lives of everyone around you to see beyond "reality" into the world of possibility.

When you dedicate every day to making the world a better place with your positive attitude and your willingness to be helpful to others, the end of your day can be met with complete and total satisfaction. Humans are designed as expansive creators of life. And, through the use of this Tool, we can accomplish great things that bring even greater internal freedom.

Your Creative Genius Within

The Tools of Creation may seem simple, they may even seem obvious. But, if creating is simple, why do we see so much suffering across so many different cultures and people?

In consideration of this fact, let's take one more look at bravery. Whether the motivation is divine or desperation, the individual may find power, often times buried within, to direct and dictate their own life's direction.

The Tools of Creation are powerful, but most effective when combined with the steady practice of all the GOGI Life Tools.

In review, the Tools of the Body empower you to take control of the physical. Tools of Choice permit you to direct your next steps along your journey. Tools of Moving Forward free you from attachments to the past. And, our beloved Tools of Creation unlock your creative genius to contribute positively to the world in which you live.

How different would your life be if you truly believed in your ability to create your life experience? Your thoughts, words, and actions are the ingredients of your creation.

Chapter 16
WHAT IF

WHAT IF is part of the set of Tools called Tools of Creation. This Tool lets you create new outcomes for yourself by taking you out of life's victim seat and putting you in charge of your decisions. You can filter everything through this Tool so you can see just where your choices are leading you. WHAT IF you signed up for a class? WHAT IF you didn't? WHAT IF you made that phone call? WHAT IF you didn't? WHAT IF you reached out to someone in need? WHAT IF you didn't?

When you start using WHAT IF for all your choices, you may first notice that most of your choices today are exactly the same as your choices yesterday. How are you expecting a different outcome with the same choices?

With this Tool, you can give all thoughts, words, and actions the WHAT IF and create something different from the past.

There are two ways you can use the Tool WHAT IF: you can use it to play out the likely results of a negative action, or you can use it to play out the positive possibilities.

What might be possible if you asked WHAT IF? WHAT IF you went back to school? WHAT IF you created a different affiliation? WHAT IF you joined AA? WHAT IF you attended chapel services? WHAT IF you read positive books? WHAT IF you didn't do the same old things? WHAT IF you learned a new skill? WHAT IF you began to work out and eat healthy foods each day?

On the other hand, WHAT IF you keep doing what you have always done? WHAT IF you don't do things differently?

Your Future Your Way

Many individuals fail to look far enough into the future to get a clear picture of the ripple effect created by every decision. As a GOGI Life Tool, WHAT IF permits you to see the likely outcome of current choices, giving you a clearer idea about what that one cigarette, that last high, or the next rage episode might mean.

Each action, as small as it may seem, has a ripple effect in your future. WHAT IF permits you to slow down your actions enough to see the future outcome of your small and seemingly insignificant decisions today.

For individuals who struggle with the desire for

the pleasure of instant gratification, or those who suffer from impulse control challenges, the Tool WHAT IF lifts the fog and lets you see the possible outcomes. You become the master, the controller, the one dictating what is going to happen to you in the future.

WHAT IF is your peek into the future and permits you to make your choices accordingly. You get to ask, "WHAT IF I am not my past?" The cool thing about the Tool WHAT IF is that it permits you to predict the likely future outcome of today's actions. If you witness someone walking into the chapel each day, the eventual outcome will likely be a person with a more religious attitude. If you witness someone pulling out a cigarette each day, the eventual outcome will be a person who hangs out with smokers, thinks about smoking, smells like smoke, and suffers from the inevitable health limitations caused by smoking. If you see someone reading and spending time in the law library, the eventual outcome will be a person with increased knowledge of law.

WHAT IF is a Tool that gets you beyond the immediate desires running rampant in your mind and has you to play out the scene like a movie script. You can ask yourself, "WHAT IF I do this? Is it negative or positive? WHAT IF I don't do this? What else might I do?"

Taming the Wave

Impulsive, frightened, angry, and depressed people all have a difficult time controlling the immediacy of their feelings. It is often difficult for them to actually see beyond the wave of emotions or opinions far enough to see an outcome.

WHAT IF is a popular Tool for anyone interested in directing their future. By looking into the possible future outcomes and by gauging if an action is on a positive or negative path, you are more inclined to overcome the wave of emotions clouding your ability to make positive decisions.

Negative? Positive?

Here is the place where people get tripped up with the Tool WHAT IF: for some reason, they refuse to acknowledge that everything they do has negative or positive implications. One more drink is negative. One more negative statement is negative. One missed AA meeting, one skipped church meeting, one time cheating on an exam, one purchase of a counterfeit certificate, one misrepresentation of the truth, are all negative.

These small and seemingly insignificant negatives create negative outcomes, much like boulders in the way of your success. Boulders which are, by the way, put in place by you.

Here is a question for you to consider: WHAT IF you stop being your only enemy and start using the Tool WHAT IF to direct every action every day? WHAT IF you did not make that poor choice you knew would only lead down a dark path? WHAT IF enough was truly enough and you got down to the business of making your life a positive creation?

WHAT IF
What If I Am Not My Past?
No to the past = Yes to the future

WHAT IF is a Tool that can be used to predict possible future outcomes. You can predict much of your future with WHAT IF. Here is how:

- **POSITIVE OR NEGATIVE?** – Is this action positive or negative?
- **BEST OR WORST?** – What is the possible outcome? What is the worst that can happen? What is the best that can happen?
- **POSSIBLE OUTCOME** – I can clearly see a potential outcome. My choice will lead me in a definite direction.
- **TAKE ACTION** – If not in a positive direction, I tell myself to pick any other action which is positive.

Your future is predictable. What you do today creates your future. WHAT IF is a Tool you can use to dedicate yourself to a positive outcome. WHAT IF there is a new you emerging, thought by thought, word by word, and action by action?

~ GOGI Coach Taylor

The GOGI Life Tools

BOSS OF MY BRAIN ✓
BELLY BREATHING ✓
FIVE SECOND LIGHTSWITCH ✓
POSITIVE THOUGHTS ✓
POSITIVE WORDS ✓
POSITIVE ACTIONS ✓
CLAIM RESPONSIBILITY ✓
LET GO ✓
FOR-GIVE ✓
WHAT IF ✓

REALITY CHECK
ULTIMATE FREEDOM

Chapter 17
REALITY CHECK

REALITY CHECK is part of the set of Tools called Tools of Creation. This Tool is your permission to be a flawed human, but does not give you permission to remain in a flawed state. Your Ten Steps Forward and Two Steps Back are still Eight Steps Ahead. Your Two Steps Back do not mean you are a failure.

Growth and change is rarely a linear process, and this Tool helps you quickly get back on track. When you use REALITY CHECK, you acknowledge you messed up, but you get back on track by making your very next decision the most positive decision possible. With REALITY CHECK, you understand that you are not perfect, but you keep moving forward toward positive growth with your very next thought, word, and action.

Using this Tool, you come to understand that your mistakes do not define you. What defines you is how you get back on track once mistakes are made.

Therefore, the GOGI Life Tool REALITY CHECK offers you a new way of thinking about change. REALITY CHECK lets you "course correct" quickly.

What often happens is that we make serious promises to stop doing something. We may even do a great job at our new commitment. Then, the bottom falls out of our lives, and something terrible happens. Somehow, we find ourselves right back into old behaviors. Or, maybe the bottom doesn't fall out, and somehow we have slipped back into our old habits without even knowing what happened.

Regardless of how we get there, many people throw in the towel and beat themselves up with shame and blame when they relapse into old behavior. Then, having given up, they decide they may as well go on another run and ride this old rodeo all the way out once again.

Stop the Ride

REALITY CHECK permits you to stop the inevitable ride to the bottom by focusing on your successes. Is it terrible that you were backsliding? Yes. But, not as terrible as giving up and letting a mistake or failure take you all the way down to rock bottom once again.

The Tool REALITY CHECK states that Ten Steps Forward and Two Steps Back is still Eight Steps Ahead. Getting back on track as quickly as possible is more important than trying to ignore or just "go with" your failures. You and everyone you know are simply human. Humans are error-prone beings in a state of constant learning.

Once you accept that learning from errors can be an opportunity throughout the human experience, you can be a little kinder to yourself when you stumble. And, you can use REALITY CHECK to get back on track quickly. There is no point in trying to be perfect. You will fail at that. There is great accomplishment, however, in not letting your failures or mistakes diminish your commitment to be your best and develop and grow your skills.

REALITY CHECK allows you to look at mistakes from the perspective that the mistake does not dictate your future success. With REALITY CHECK, you get right back on track as quickly as possible and keep moving forward.

As with all the GOGI Life Tools, our interpretation of the actual words are different than the common use of the words. FOR–GIVE, for example, is different than the act of forgiving. As a Tool, CLAIM RESPONSIBILITY is different than claiming responsibility. This is similar with REALITY CHECK.

Never Perfect Always Progress

REALITY CHECK is a Tool for you to use when you backstep, make a mistake, fall off, do something stupid, or are tempted to toss in the towel and focus on your imperfections. With the Tool REALITY CHECK, you understand you are not perfect. You will never be perfect, but you can strive for the most perfect version of you.

If perfection is something you attempt to achieve in vain, you may find yourself in a downward spiral of self-hatred sinking further into bad decisions because you are discouraged by your imperfections.

REALITY CHECK is about not falling victim to the perfection syndrome, but rather, remaining focused on getting back on the right path as quickly as possible so the damage done by poor choices is as minimal as possible.

Your Life Raft

As a Tool, REALITY CHECK can be used as a life raft in the sea of bad decisions. It is your escape route from needing one more rodeo ride. It is your ticket back on the right track, back to the positive choices you have made and will continue to make. REALITY CHECK does not focus on your mistakes, but focuses on how much good you have done up to the time of your mistake. Then, setting the mistakes aside, REALITY CHECK has you focus on getting right back on track with the use of your GOGI Life Tools.

Remember, if you take Ten Steps Forward and then fall back a couple steps, you are still Eight Steps Ahead. If you take Ten Steps Forward and eleven steps back, at least you know how to take a step forward.

There is no room for self victimization with REALITY CHECK because you are not going to sit around and beat yourself up with negative self talk. With this Tool, you are able to pick yourself up and decide your next positive action.

Delicate Dance of Change

REALITY CHECK is an awesome Tool because change is rarely linear. It is almost always a delicate dance of backward and forward, inching your way into a new reality. Of course, it is easier if we just walk the path forward; But, alas, humans are humans and it appears as if we prefer to learn things the hard way until we decide the easy way is... easier. REALITY CHECK permits us to create an easier route toward change in the dance of creating a positive life.

As hard as you try, you will never find perfection in this lifetime.

We are human and being human is a learning experience. Realizing this, we may apply the GOGI Life Tool called REALITY CHECK to our learning process.

Remember, ten steps forward and two steps back is still eight steps ahead!

REALITY CHECK
Ten And Two Rule
Ten Steps Forward and Two Steps Back is still Eight Steps Ahead.

REALITY CHECK is your Tool for when you mess up, make a mistake, or fall victim to temptation. REALITY CHECK also helps you have compassion for weaknesses in others. It works like this:

- **FACT** – I messed up.

- **PROGRESS** – There are many times I don't mess up. I have made progress. I have done really well, better than I have in the past. One mistake does not erase all the good I have done. I understand my good is still good.

- **BACK ON TRACK** – Right now, in this moment, I can choose more good, adding to the list of good things I have done. I commit to POSITIVE ACTIONS right now. I am back on track.

REALITY CHECK is the perfect Tool if shame, self-loathing, embarrassment, and discouragement have been your pattern. You are not and will never be perfect, but you can commit to being better today than yesterday, and better tomorrow than today.

~ GOGI Coach Taylor

Chapter 18
ULTIMATE FREEDOM

ULTIMATE FREEDOM is part of the set of Tools called Tools of Creation. This Tool is the least obvious of the Tools because it is used to create a way of moving through your day and not necessarily a Tool you pull out when something breaks down. When you use your Tool ULTIMATE FREEDOM, you make decisions that help you be of service to others.

You use this Tool by being positive; that is a service to others. You do this by being helpful; that is a service to others. You do this by being a safe distance from harm; that is a service to others.

When you use ULTIMATE FREEDOM, you realize that you are important and a potential solution to any and every problem. As a walking and talking potential solution, you are living a life of service. THAT is the ultimate use of the Tool ULTIMATE FREEDOM.

ULTIMATE FREEDOM is pretty simple: until you

are living each and every day of your life in service, making the world a better place, you are not truly free. If you are living for your own gratification, you will eventually become aware that there is more to life.

If you are living your life to "get more" and "have more" then you will eventually experience disappointment and dissatisfaction. ULTIMATE FREEDOM, as a GOGI Life Tool, helps us realize our freedom is not determined by physical freedom.

ULTIMATE FREEDOM is what can be experienced when you focus your life's actions toward helping others and living humbly in service of those who struggle. You develop compassion for those who remain blinded by the need for "things" or the need to maintain a certain image.

Live With No Regrets

When, at the end of the day, you can review your activities and decisions and count numerous times that you brought a smile or hope to another individual, that is when you can be certain that this Tool, ULTIMATE FREEDOM, is part of your every day life.

Living your life in humble service and making your corner of the world a nicer, cleaner, and a kinder place permits your life to be filled with learning, sharing, and loving.

When we get close to the time we leave this earth, we will naturally reflect on important things that have defined our lives. In speaking with thousands of individuals who suffer from illnesses that will one day take their life, they consistently speak about relationships, learning, sharing, and communication being the most important. A dying individual simply does not talk about big houses, new cars, and all the distractions which are promoted in our culture as the route to happiness. A dying individual will tell you about love, regrets in love, the importance of the small things in life, and the small acts of kindness they experienced. They often speak of regrets.

So, while we have thousands upon thousands of individuals who, on their death beds, have told us what is truly important, why is it that we focus on the superficial collection of things we cannot take with us when we leave this earth? Using ULTIMATE FREEDOM, you can experience compassion for those who suffer in a prison of their mind.

Your Freedom

Knowing that sustained internal freedom is strengthened through service, your focus would likely be on building positive connections with those around you.

Using your Tool ULTIMATE FREEDOM will help you focus your efforts on choices that benefit your life, as well as the lives of others. This is how you earn lifelong respect as someone who contributes more than they consume. You become trusted this way. You experience love this way.

The Tool ULTIMATE FREEDOM makes internal freedom possible for each one of us. The other GOGI

Life Tools are simply Tools to position us to live a life where we use the Tool ULTIMATE FREEDOM daily. By using your Tools and being of service at least one time each day, you are inching your way toward truly living a life of internal freedom.

Service as a Key

There is likely no greater internal joy than living your life in the service of those in need, but (and there is always a but) this cannot be done until you are in the mental and emotional space to actually be of service. If you are not prepared to be of service, you may measure and count your service and indebt others in your mind. When this happens, you are still in a form of a prison.

The Tool ULTIMATE FREEDOM is certainly not for the faint of heart or those clouded with the need to be acknowledged or rewarded. ULTIMATE FREEDOM is about doing something for others, something which will probably never be noticed.

Better yet, do something positive for others who have harmed, hurt, or caused you pain. Be of service to anyone, regardless of their actions towards you. This will give you a freedom few others experience.

Simple Freedom

This may be quite a heavy concept to grasp so let's keep it simple; let's keep it to the daily actions you choose in your life. By committing to doing one act of kindness for another human being, which is not seen nor heard by others, you are laying the foundation for a life filled with the freedom for which we all strive, freedom within.

We all want to be internally free of sadness, anger, codependency, dependence, depression, addiction, rage, despair, hopelessness, illness, etc. A true balm for these feelings, a lasting healing, comes from the daily practice of the Tool ULTIMATE FREEDOM.

It is not necessary to picture yourself being of service by roaming the country in long robes and picking up trash along the freeways for the rest of your life. Begin to think about how you can use ULTIMATE FREEDOM today, in simple ways. Pick out one little, seemingly insignificant, thing you can do to make the life of someone else just a little bit better. Do that thing without any expectation of acknowledgment, reward, or privilege. Do it unnoticed. Do it, just to do it. If someone says thank you or notices you, pick out something else you can do where there is no reward, no "thank you" attached.

Maybe it is as simple as picking up a piece of trash or making the row of books a little more organized. Maybe it is keeping your bedding tidy and nice to look at or teaching someone to read. Maybe it is writing a letter of gratitude (or apology) to a teacher at your high school or sharing inspiring words with the students of that school.

Whatever it is, pick one way in which you can be of service. Fill your life with these acts and freedom will be your lasting life experience, regardless of the inevitable challenges you will face.

ULTIMATE FREEDOM

Being Free Is Up To Me
Living a Life of Service Sets me Internally Free

ULTIMATE FREEDOM is a "state of being" just as much as it is a Tool. Here is how to practice the Tool ULTIMATE FREEDOM each and every day:

- **FREE DAY** – I begin my day in freedom from anything which might hold me back. Today, I am of positive service to the world.

- **SERVICE** – I will do one thing for which I accept no money and will accumulate no favors. If possible, I will do this act of service without anyone knowing.

- **JOY** – I will slow my thoughts enough to feel the joy in my heart that only comes from doing good deeds today.

- **SMILE** – Even if things are terrible in my life right now, I will smile each and every time I think about ULTIMATE FREEDOM and my service to the world.

- **END EACH DAY** – I end my day by reviewing times I used ULTIMATE FREEDOM, when I was in service. Being of service sets me internally free!

Chapter 19
Putting Your Tools to Use

Notes & Suggestions from
GOGI Coach Taylor

As you come to the end of this book you may have many questions. A couple may be how to use your GOGI Life Tools, and what level of impact might they have in your life. In this chapter, we will review some of the questions students have asked over the years. The first of which is how to use the GOGI Life Tools.

Using Your GOGI Life Tools

As an individual, you can use your GOGI Life Tools in any way they work for you. If you were a car mechanic, you could use your tools anyway that works to fix the problem at hand. There are, of course, general tendencies and suggested uses, but your goal is to get the job done your way. You do not need to try to do things the way a to-do manual claims is the "correct way." You can observe others, test tools, practice options, and figure things out for yourself. Or, you can follow the manual and reduce the trial and error process.

The point is, these are now your Tools. Some individuals follow the GOGI Life Tool Calendar and find comfort in the knowledge they are never alone in their study of the GOGI Life Tools. Other individuals don't pay any attention to the calendar, and, in fact, don't even use all the Tools. For some, maybe one Tool is their go-to Tool and that's all they need. The point is, all ways to use the GOGI Life Tools are correct.

The goal of the GOGI Life Tools is to help anyone, anywhere, make more positive decisions. This means that anyone, anywhere, can use the Tools anyway that supports their positive decision making process. Remember, too, that ULTIMATE FREEDOM suggests that being free is a choice you can make, and living with a perspective of service strengthens the freedom process. When you live your life with compassion for the perspectives and experiences of others, your freedom will grow within you, and you will find yourself sharing your GOGI Life Tools with others.

Help Others

While you may not feel sufficiently trained, adequately educated, or prepared to facilitate the sharing of the GOGI Life Tools with others, it is precisely through sharing that your education becomes solidified. Sharing a thought, an idea, or a concept does not require expertise, you do not need to be an expert. It simply requires experience. When you approach sharing your Tools with this perspective, you will find deep connections rooted in the humanity we all share.

Helping others is not a job for experts as much as it is for like minded individuals who have experienced a similar journey. At GOGI, we have always held the most value in the experience of the student, realizing that the student is actually the best teacher.

When you feel motivated to discuss your Tools, please do not hesitate. Somewhere along the way someone will need to hear the exact words you share. Even if your words are not perfect, they might help lighten someone's load, just as yours was lightened.

Help Yourself

Remember, too, that with your focus on service to others, you are doing yourself the greatest service. As you engage in helping others with a smile or a simple act of friendship, you will have no time to wallow in the challenges or the impossibility of your situation. Your focus will be on the suffering of others and the simple ways you can help nudge others to a more positive perspective. This distraction from your own struggles will help you put your struggles into perspective, and your load will be lightened.

Over time, with a focus on helping make the world a more pleasant place, you may discover that your concerns are not as heavy as you had previously perceived. The key is for you to look within for your answers and realize that within is where you find the strength to be of service to others.

Continue Your Study

This book is designed to be informative, but it can

be an ongoing source of inspiration and instruction. This book may help you to revisit time and time again the function of each Tool and the new ways you can apply them to the inevitable challenges you face. In this book is sufficient information to hold a weekly GOGI Meeting or a study group. You can make copies of pages of this book to share with others. You can even encourage others to engage in the book report options and enjoy the handouts in the back of this book.

This book can be whatever you wish it to be. Remember, GOGI is your set of Tools to help you create the kind of life you always wanted but lacked the Tools to create.

Creating Your Life the GOGI Way

When we are young we don't see the end of our life clearly. As we age, as we mature, the end of our life becomes something that crosses our mind more frequently. As we become old, we glance back at our life and begin to reflect. Regardless of the decisions you have made in your past, at any point you can decide that the present is the best day to make the most positive decisions. Living each day in this manner will permit you to glance back at your life from the perspective of the progress you made, rather than regrets that you accumulate.

Sometimes, when working with a young group of students, I will ask them to write what their eulogy might say. Most of them don't know what a eulogy is or how to write it, but once I tell them it is something read at their funeral, they begin the reflection process. As you think about your own life, there will be those who remain hurt by your actions, but likely many more who were blessed by your presence. If you think of your own eulogy and the lives you positively impacted, your choices today and the words you choose may alter a bit.

Another activity I challenge my students to complete is the "unwritten letter" assignment, whereby I ask the student to write a letter to someone they have failed to write, but someone who needs to hear from them. This is most often a series of letters written to family who have been betrayed or friends who have been harmed. But in all cases, the Student of GOGI is able to share that they have new Tools with which they can now make more positive decisions.

Reflection is required for you to chart your course to a positive direction. Without reflection, we have a tendency to repeat the past. The GOGI Life Tools can help you function more solidly, and your thoughtful introspection will speak to your heart as to what they mean in your life. This can be done during sincere conversations with like minded individuals, support groups, therapy, prayer, or other studies. What will not work for you is running away, numbing the pain, and pretending the hurt does not hurt.

From all the volunteers at GOGI (and we are all volunteers at GOGI), we invite you to venture into the type of life you may never have thought possible, a type of life that makes the world a better place, just because you are on it.

Ways to Study GOGI

GOGI Meetings

In my 20 years as a volunteer inside prisons and jails, I have witnessed dozens, if not hundreds, of instances where rival gang members and former enemies gather to share the GOGI Life Tools in the safe and supportive environment GOGI Meetings provide. I have seen color lines, along with all other exclusionary criteria, otherwise defining who is a friend and who is not, evaporate when the focus becomes being of service to community.

The world we can build for all humanity is not some far off dream. Rather, it is the world in which I live every day of my life. I witness positive choices being made through utilization of the GOGI Life Tools inside some of the most notorious prisons across the United States of America.

GOGI Meetings have a way of inspiring a powerfully positive community. The GOGI Life Tools quickly find a home within the hearts of those who engage in the study of GOGI. GOGI Meetings offer the format, the permission, and even the excuse for each individual to be magnificent, and they are free.

GOGI Meetings Emerge

GOGI Meetings are the vision of Students of GOGI who believe that when united in a common language of positive decision-making, there is nothing a community is unable to accomplish. The GOGI Life Tools offer you and your community the permission to get out of your own way and unite with others in one great cause of living a purposeful life path.

GOGI's Roots ~ GOGI at the Bay

In 2015, Getting Out by Going In received grant funding to provide "programming" to prisoners in the highest security housing units of Pelican Bay State Prison (PBSP) and California Corrections Institution (CCI).

Walking from one cell to the next with a push-cart overflowing with GOGI course workbooks, I was able to convince maximum security prisoners to simply "look" at the GOGI material, even if they had not been offered or had refused rehabilitative programs before.

Month after month I would return, distributing more and more courses as word spread throughout Pelican Bay State Prison that GOGI was the real deal. Once the reality of GOGI offering simple Tools caught on, I would hear one prisoner giving a head's up to cells down the hall. "GOGI's in the house, you better have your homework ready." The men would holler this out, notifying the others down the line that GOGI Coach Taylor or another GOGI representative had been permitted in the unit.

Air Vent Meetings

I remember one time I made it into the housing unit without the normal fanfare of being noticed and my arrival being announced. I walked into the housing unit of CCI in their maximum security housing. With my officer escort, I made my way to one of the cells where a very enthusiastic Student of GOGI was housed. Upon my approach, I heard him speaking. I immediately wondered if he had smuggled a cell phone, as that was increasingly common. I hoped I was not going to be walking up to a situation I did not want to see. I stood back a few feet and listened before approaching.

The Student of GOGI was on his top bunk. His mouth was as close to the air vent as possible. He was talking about GOGI. I was curious. He was single-celled and had no one else in the cell with him. I glanced into the adjacent cell. Sure enough, the guy next door was in the same position. Two men were actually talking about GOGI.

"Are you two men holding a GOGI meeting?" I asked, as I approached his cell door.

"Coach Taylor, you can't walk up on people like that," came his startled reply.

"Yeah, sorry about that, but I was hearing some GOGI talk and couldn't resist."

As it turned out, since the men were not permitted to be out of their cells at the same time due to their security level, they had formed their very own meetings through the air vents to enhance their ability to make positive decisions. They were not alone in their desire to make big changes in their lives. An increasing number of high security prisons were finding freedom, the GOGI Way.

Housing Unit Meetings

At Pelican Bay, it was not uncommon for one of the men in a unit to hold a GOGI Meeting loud enough for the men in adjacent cells to chime in with their own contributions. At the Bay, SHU housing configurations were modular in format, but the cell bars within each module made open discussions possible. Men in their cells reviewed their materials and conducted very organized and well-documented meetings. These men were able to hold GOGI Meetings and create a positive environment that promoted growth and insight development.

As these higher security prisoners transitioned to less restrictive housing, they continued with their GOGI study, inviting others to join in this new "GOGI Culture," as they called it. GOGI became the new way of navigating life on the prison yard.

Many Meeting Configurations

Meetings with like-minded individuals are most often created by student's eagerness to share and explore the application of the GOGI Life Tools. Rare is it to find someone who does not want to speak about, share, and exemplify the GOGI Life Tools once they find them useful in their own lives.

Students of GOGI tried, tested, and explored the optimal way to empower communities for good. Through their contributions, the GOGI Meetings were created. The Students of GOGI wish the gift of internal freedom to be yours.

Your Opportunity

It is my sincere hope that you found value in the material offered throughout the chapters of this book. It certainly took years of conversations, explorations, and trial and error to offer the GOGI Life Tools in a manner in which you may find them helpful.

We sincerely hope the GOGI Life Tools become part of your every day life. From all the Students of GOGI, I can say with confidence that living the GOGI Way is a great way to live.

What are GOGI Meetings?

GOGI Meetings are positive gatherings of individuals formed in Circle Groups to reinforce daily use of the GOGI Life Tools. These meetings are ideal for those who wish to contribute to a positive community engaged in the study of the GOGI Life Tools.

A complete version of the manual is available in PDF form via email. A softbound version is available for purchase at www.gettingoutbygoingin.org/shop. In this format, the calendar is followed and the GOGI Meeting Format is offered in open or closed group format. Anyone can hold weekly GOGI Meetings.

Copies of this Manual?

Pages of this manual can be copied and shared with individuals attending your GOGI Meeting. This will help Circle Group members engage, feel included, and want to participate, and it may make the facilitators job less stressful.

Course & Topic Specific GOGI Meetings

Course Specific GOGI Meetings

Course Specific GOGI Meetings are an engaging way to enhance study of GOGI Life Tool use for specific topics. While a GOGI Group can be formed for general life improvement, a GOGI Group can also be formed to permit students to complete any one of GOGI's courses as a Circle Group. In this format, a group meets to complete a specific GOGI course.

This team-approach to complete specific courses permits a deeper engagement with the course materials and often solidifies the application of the GOGI Life Tools in specific circumstances. A GOGI Meeting with a Circle Group focused on the completion of GOGI' Addition and Substance Use course or GOGI's Anger Management Course is an ideal way to not only permit self reflection, but encourage positive peer support.

Topic Specific GOGI Meetings

Topic Specific GOGI Meetings are effective for supporting a specific challenge. A Circle Group can be formed for any number of life's challenges, with each Circle Group member focused on utilization of the GOGI Life Tools to overcome a shared challenge.

Whether a course-specific, or topic-specific approach is taken, Circle Group members are encouraged to focus intently on application of the GOGI Life Tools to resolve and overcome any of life's challenges.

Independent Correspondence Courses

All courses can be purchased by individuals or organizations. In this format, the Student of GOGI completes independent study of GOGI's workbook courses.

With an expertise in rehabilitative programming embedded in the roots of GOGI, the correspondence courses have become a beloved and effective means to prepare for success beyond prison walls, addiction, and any other challenge.

Below are covers of GOGI's most popular correspondence courses available on the GOGI website: www.gettingoutbygoingin.org

Leadership Training Programs

In Leadership Training Programs, participants are able to increase their ability to be of service through structured requirements. Each certification requires specific study, all culminating in certification as a Certified GOGI Coach. GOGI Leadership Training Programs were created in collaboration with tens of thousands of Students of GOGI who were committed to providing their families, friends, and communities with a lasting solution for the challenges they faced.

Over a twenty year period, many different leadership styles and formats were integrated into the all-inclusive leadership formats currently offered by GOGI. Below is a short recap of levels of engagement and certifications offered to support milestones in GOGI course completions.

GOGI Coach Certification

Certifying as a GOGI Coach requires a 2-year process and 35 GOGI academic course credits. Also required is a 30-page thesis project. The GOGI Coach is the highest honor in the GOGI Leadership Training Program and acknowledges the individual as having met the highest criteria required by the GOGI organization.

GOGI Peer Coach

The GOGI Peer Coach has completed required GOGI courses and has displayed an interest in mentoring or supporting GOGI Life Tool studies in a group setting. The GOGI Peer Coach was once a GOGI Ambassador, then G-Rep, then Facilitator of GOGI Meetings.

As a GOGI Peer Coach, they are encouraged to support group study of the GOGI Life Tools.

GOGI Facilitator Certification

The GOGI Facilitator has completed the G-Rep Certification and has assisted in the facilitation of two cycles of GOGI Meetings.

GOGI G-Rep

A G-Rep is a person who has completed the basic GOGI training for leadership which may be offered in workshop or course format. As a G-Rep, this individual is well versed in their GOGI Life Tools and confident in sharing those Tools with friends and family.

They may assist in GOGI Meetings or advocate for the sharing of the GOGI Life Tools within their community.

GOGI Ambassador

A GOGI Ambassador is anyone who finds the GOGI Life Tools supportive of positive decision making. This individual advocates for the use of the GOGI Life Tools for all communities and is able to share their support of GOGI Life Tools as a universal language of positive decision making.

Build Your Confidence as a GOGI Meeting Facilitator

The first thing to understand is that anyone can lead a GOGI Meeting. Each meeting has the same outline. Every week a specific Tool is studied. Once you are familiar with the format, your confidence in facilitating GOGI Meetings will grow. That being said, here are some specific focus points when considering facilitating GOGI Meetings.

___ Are the members of the meeting sitting in Peer Circles of no more than 12 members?

___ As the facilitator, am I listening more than I am speaking? A good facilitator will always listen more than they speak.

___ Is the meeting I am facilitating focused on the Tool of the week according to the GOGI Life Tool Calendar?

___ Are members of the meeting clear about credits? Or, no credits? Or, requirements for the group?

___ Am I able to provide each Circle Group with adequate handouts or copies of official GOGI material?

___ Am I securing volunteers for the next week? A good facilitator will ask for volunteers for the upcoming meeting.

___ Do all people feel welcome into the GOGI Meetings? A good facilitator provides an inclusive environment that benefits everyone.

GOGI Correspondence Courses

Earn an official GOGI Certificate with completion of each course.

Getting Out by Going In offers many ways to study the GOGI Life Tools. Below are just a few of the courses available for individual and group course study.

For more information visit www.GettingOutByGoingIn.org
Or write to GOGI, PO Box 88969, Los Angeles, CA 90009

GOGI Meeting
Essentials

How to Get Your Meeting Started

Sign Up Sheets

GOGI Meetings are most often formed through a sign-up form. Willing participation is ideal for GOGI Meetings. No one should be required to join a GOGI Meeting. Once a group is established, new members can be admitted as needed to replace those who are no longer participating.

What is a Circle Group?

A Circle Group is no more than twelve participants in a closed circle. When there are thirteen members, the Circle Group is split and two Circle Groups are formed. The entire GOGI Meeting can be as large as the meeting space allows; however, the Circle Groups are 2-12 individuals in size. No Circle Group should be larger than 12 participants or smaller than 5 members. For example, there have been more than 300 participants who have met in one space and formed 30 Circle Groups for their GOGI Meeting.

Forming a Circle Group

The most productive Circle Groups are often self-selected. Self-selection includes peer referral, word of mouth, and peer invitation. Permitting individuals an opportunity to circle with like-minded peers often proves more successful than when Circle Groups are formed without the benefit of positive prior relationships.

If self-selection is not possible, a shared experience group is another option. These individuals may have a shared goal, shared life experience, or similar situation. The shared experience model permits the focus of the meetings to be relevant to Circle Group members' experience.

What is a Meeting Cycle?

Each GOGI Meeting Cycle consists of 15 Meetings. A cycle includes a Team Building Meeting, 12 Tool Meetings, a Tool Review Meeting, and a Celebrate Success Meeting.

Credit or No Credit?

Is attendance credit given for GOGI Meetings?

If you are attending a GOGI Meeting inside of a school or institution or if the group is sponsored by an organization, it is likely that your attendance is being tracked. The hosting organization might even provide attendance credit or a completion certificate of some sort.

Are certifications given for completing GOGI Meeting Cycles?

In many cases, participants hope to be acknowledged for more than simply attending GOGI Meetings. Credit is especially valuable in instances where a certificate or grade can document the level of comprehension in application of the GOGI Life Tools.

Does GOGI issue credit for GOGI Meetings?

While GOGI does not track attendance or provide credit for GOGI Meetings, tracking attendance and the issuance of certifications is encouraged at the local level. GOGI does not issue these types of credits for GOGI Meetings, even if quizzes or reports are completed. Credit is at the local level.

When does GOGI issue credit?

GOGI issues formal GOGI credits when published softbound workbooks are completed and submitted to our organization for academic review. These courses are categorized as "Correspondence Courses." GOGI does not track meetings, as those are intended to be an open-source and free format offered to any group wishing to support the learning of GOGI Life Tools.

What kinds of acknowledgment is appropriate?

Attendance is the easiest acknowledgement to track and easiest to award in situations where administrative assistance is limited. Sign in/sign out sheets are often used to document attendance.

Student attendance cards are another simple way

to track attendance. Each student brings a GOGI Meeting Attendance Card or other attendance tracking document to each meeting. A staff member or supervisor documenting attendance signs this document every meeting to keep track of attendance.

The goal of the GOGI Life Tools is to empower all individuals to realize they can create their own positive life experience through use of the GOGI Life Tools. By offering GOGI Meetings as a free, volunteer-run, community facilitated option for individuals and organizations, GOGI reaches its mission and vision for a better world for all mankind. The GOGI Life Tools are free, fun, and meant to be shared.

Group Success Checklist

You know your GOGI Meeting is the best it can be when you can say yes to all the below:

Seating

✓ Are all Circle Group members seated in a circle?

✓ Have all desks or tables been moved out of the way so chairs permit a circle to be created?

✓ Can all Circle Group members see each other?

Participation

✓ Are all members of the group attending willingly?

✓ Are Circle Groups 2-12 members?

✓ Do participants have access to GOGI materials?

Format

✓ Do all Circle Groups have names and guidelines?

✓ Does the larger group break into Circle Groups at the beginning of the meeting?

✓ Do all Circle Groups follow the GOGI Life Tool Calendar?

✓ Do all Circle Groups hold the Team Building Meeting at the completion of each cycle (15 Meetings)?

Leaders

✓ Are the facilitators encouraging volunteerism within the Circle Group?

✓ Are the facilitators asking more questions than they offer statements?

✓ Are the facilitators keeping the Circle Group on time and on format?

Calendar

✓ Is the Circle Group on Calendar?

✓ Is the Circle Group prepared for the Tool Review and Celebrate Success Meetings?

✓ Is the Circle Group prepared for holding the Team Building Meeting to start the next cycle?

GOGI Meeting Format

On the following pages is the format for GOGI Meetings.

Consult your GOGI Life Tool Calendar to determine which Tool should be your focus each week.

Administrative Duties and Details

If there are announcements, administrative details, voting, or distribution of materials, these tasks are to be conducted before your meeting begins.

1) Group Circles *(read aloud)*

"GOGI Meetings and all GOGI studies are defined by our GOGI Life Tool Calendar and our groups. If we have not already done so, at this time we break from the larger group meeting into our groups of 2-12 participants."

2) Start Your Meeting *(read aloud)*

"The GOGI Life Tools are studied worldwide according to the GOGI Life Tool Calendar. We unite with others according to this schedule, so no one will feel they are alone in their effort to make positive decisions. We believe in everyone's ability to benefit from this positive community of individuals united in the GOGI Life Tool Calendar. Therefore, we call this GOGI (The Tool You Are Studying) Meeting to order, and we join in the Tool being studied by Students of GOGI everywhere."

3) Review of The GOGI Life Tools *(read aloud)*

BOSS OF MY BRAIN
BELLY BREATHING
FIVE SECOND LIGHTSWITCH
POSITIVE THOUGHTS
POSITIVE WORDS
POSITIVE ACTIONS
CLAIM RESPONSIBILITY
LET GO
FOR-GIVE
WHAT IF
REALITY CHECK
ULTIMATE FREEDOM

4) The GOGI Purpose *(volunteer to read)*

"The objective of GOGI Meetings is to reinforce the use of the GOGI Life Tools and support positive community experiences. We accomplish our objective through the study of the GOGI Life Tools shared in Circle Groups according to the GOGI Life Tool Calendar."

5) Group Check-In

Each member may be given the opportunity to "check-in," stating one positive thing that happened during the week.

6) Tool Reading *(Volunteer/s to Share)*

A volunteer may choose from the Tool information shared in with group members. Not all the information needs to be read aloud. Additional

Tool information from any of the GOGI books, courses, newsletters, or open source materials can be used to help clarify Tool use options.

Tool Objective ~ Tool Statement of Ownership ~ Tool Keywords ~ Tool Basics

Ask a Tool Specific Thought Provoking Question

- When was the last time you used (the Tool of the Week)? Did you know you were using this Tool?

- Do you believe there is value in teaching children (the Tool of the week)? Explain.

- What might have been different in your life had you been taught to use (the Tool of the week) in your childhood?

- How would you explain this Tool to a close friend? What would you say were the benefits?

7) Applying the Tool *(group member discussion)*

Members of the group are invited to share personal experiences related to this week's Tool. Challenges in applying the Tool are also discussed. Open dialogue includes all group members in equal sharing of talk time.

8) Optional Tool Activity

Understanding that activities often reinforce group members' engagement and understanding of the GOGI Life Tools, now is a great time to engage in an activity which can be created by the group, gleaned from the GOGI materials, or utilized in prior GOGI Groups.

9) Weekly Statement of Intention

Each member of the group is encouraged to complete this sentence: "It is my intention this week to _____."

10) The GOGI Pledge of Service *(read aloud)*

"All Students of GOGI unite with our GOGI Pledge of Service. This pledge defines our purpose and is repeated at the end of every GOGI Meeting. Remaining in your Circle Groups, each group will rotate leading the pledge for the larger group. As we close this GOGI Meeting, we unite as a community with our pledge to be of service. Please repeat after me:

May our commitment (repeat)
To the study of GOGI (repeat)
Grant us the joy (repeat)
Of giving and receiving (repeat)
So that our inner freedom (repeat)
May be of maximum service (repeat)
To those we love (repeat)
And infinite others (repeat)"

11) Tidy Up Time *(read aloud)*

"We thank you for participating in this week's GOGI Meeting. Our next meeting will be held (day/time/place) and the Tool to be discussed according to the GOGI Calendar will be the Tool (refer to calendar). If holding a meeting in one room, please let us leave this room clean and tidy for the next group."

GOGI Life Tool Calendar

According to the calendar, each week starts on Monday. The first Monday of each month begins that month's study. When there is a 5th Monday, all the Tools can be reviewed during that week.

January

Week 1 BOSS OF MY BRAIN

Week 2 BELLY BREATHING

Week 3 FIVE SECOND LIGHTSWITCH

Week 4 POSITIVE THOUGHTS

February

Week 1 POSITIVE WORDS

Week 2 POSITIVE ACTIONS

Week 3 CLAIM RESPONSIBILITY

Week 4 LET GO

March

Week 1 FOR-GIVE

Week 2 WHAT IF

Week 3 REALITY CHECK

Week 4 ULTIMATE FREEDOM

April

Week 1 BOSS OF MY BRAIN

Week 2 BELLY BREATHING

Week 3 FIVE SECOND LIGHTSWITCH

Week 4 POSITIVE THOUGHTS

May

Week 1 POSITIVE WORDS

Week 2 POSITIVE ACTIONS

Week 3 CLAIM RESPONSIBILITY

Week 4 LET GO

June

Week 1 FOR-GIVE

Week 2 WHAT IF

Week 3 REALITY CHECK

Week 4 ULTIMATE FREEDOM

July

Week 1 BOSS OF MY BRAIN

Week 2 BELLY BREATHING

Week 3 FIVE SECOND LIGHTSWITCH

Week 4 POSITIVE THOUGHTS

August

Week 1 POSITIVE WORDS

Week 2 POSITIVE ACTIONS

Week 3 CLAIM RESPONSIBILITY

Week 4 LET GO

September

Week 1 FOR-GIVE

Week 2 WHAT IF

Week 3 REALITY CHECK

Week 4 ULTIMATE FREEDOM

October

Week 1 BOSS OF MY BRAIN

Week 2 BELLY BREATHING

Week 3 FIVE SECOND LIGHTSWITCH

Week 4 POSITIVE THOUGHTS

November

Week 1 POSITIVE WORDS

Week 2 POSITIVE ACTIONS

Week 3 CLAIM RESPONSIBILITY

Week 4 LET GO

December

Week 1 FOR-GIVE

Week 2 WHAT IF

Week 3 REALITY CHECK

Week 4 ULTIMATE FREEDOM

Book Reports & Handouts

In this section, you will find opportunities to further explore what you have learned in this book and assess your comprehension. These optional assessments and assignments are tools for you to use. GOGI does not issue credit for completion of these assignments; however, a group, institution, or school may decide to award you credit. The only exception is GOGI's My Life Story Course and the Book Report, for which you will receive credit for completion when we have sufficient volunteer staff to process your credit once submitted to our Post Office Box address.

In this section, you will find:

1) **Template for Optional Verbal Quiz**

2) **Template for Optional Reflective Writing Assignment**

3) ***"GOGI Life Tools Mini Book"* Book Report:** This optional course is a 15 page reflection. When you send this completed course to GOGI, and when GOGI has sufficient volunteer staff, you will receive an official certificate of completion.

4) ***"The GOGI My Life Story Certificate Course"*:** This optional course is a 15 page reflection. When you send this completed course to GOGI, and when GOGI has sufficient volunteer staff, you will receive an official certificate of completion.

Template for Optional Verbal Quiz

This quiz is for internal or personal use only. This assessment can be used to determine if an individual is ready to help facilitate or support a GOGI Meeting. This is an easy way to assess basic comprehension of the GOGI Life Tools.

The below are suggested questions you may consider when making your own Verbal Quiz.

- What are the four sets of Tools?

- What are the names of all 12 GOGI Life Tools?

- What Tools are included in the Tools of the Body?

- What Tools are included in the Tools of Choice?

- What Tools are included in the Tools of Moving Forward?

- What Tools are included in the Tools of Creation?

- Why does GOGI have the GOGI Life Tool Calendar?

- What is your favorite Tool and why?

- In your opinion, what is the most interesting aspect of GOGI Meetings?

- Can you recite the GOGI Pledge of Service?

Template for Optional Reflective Writing Assignments

In the Reflective Writing, students reflect on what they have learned and how they can apply the GOGI Life Tools. Credit for the Reflective Writing is provided by the hosting organization. Here are some suggestions when considering Reflective Writing Assignments as a way to encourage a deeper engagement than attending the weekly meetings may offer. Creating a handout that is distributed weekly is likely to be most productive. Waiting until the end of the cycle may discourage participants.

Weekly Reflective Writing Assignment Options

Ask for their name, other information about them, including date, time, and place of the meeting.

Ask for thoughts on the Tool of the Week that was discussed during the meeting. Oftentimes, the participant can recall the Keywords and in their own words review the Statement of Purpose and objective of each Tool.

Ask the student if they have seen this Tool in action and ask them to share an example. This assesses comprehension and attention.

Permit the student to create a scenario where they would use the Tool in the future is also an enjoyable experience for participants.

Whatever is decided upon as far as requirements, it is suggested to keep the reflective writing simple, short, and weekly.

The GOGI Life Tools Mini Book

FREE GOGI COURSE

The GOGI Life Tools Mini Book
Book Report Course

Two ways to earn a certificate: **1)** Your organization or institution will collect your work and will issue credit or order the credit from GOGI. Or, **2)** You mail the completed course in 1-2 envelopes to: GOGI, PO Box 88969, Los Angeles, CA 90009. Within 6-8 weeks, GOGI mails a completion certificate.

The requirements for "*The GOGI Life Tools Mini Book*" Book Report Course are:

1) Use a standard-size paper measuring 8 inches by 10 or 8.5 inches by 11. This is the most common size of **lined school paper.**

2) Write your **first and last name and ID number** on the top of every page to ensure you are given credit for each page.

3) Make certain you include your **mailing address** at the top of the first page or your work may not be processed to your address.

4) Please **number your pages** 1-19 to help us keep your work organized.

5) **Write** your responses in **pen, pencil, or crayon**. Do not type, email, or text. Do not worry about spelling, grammar, writing style, or language. Non-English speakers may write the responses in their native language.

6) Each chapter of the book will require you to write **one full page** addressing some or all of the questions outlined in these requirements.

7) Write on both sides of the paper. This means you will complete 19 full pages of reflective writing utilizing **10 sheets of paper** to accomplish this task.

8) This course may be completed as a **group or independently**. How you complete this book report is up to you. A weekly book club or in addition to a weekly GOGI meeting are popular.

9) **Write from your heart.** GOGI will not judge you for your responses. Responses are for your personal development only. There are no right or wrong answers. The only requirement is to complete one full page of writing for each chapter.

10) **Write to your comfort level.** You are not required to write details of life events you do not want to share. There are many ways to speak about events without details. You are able to write to your comfort level. Remember, this reflective writing is for you.

> To help process your work. **Each page** should contain the following information at the top:
> 1) My name is _____   2) My ID is _____
> 3) This is page #____   4) This is chapter # ___

Use any of the questions below for your writing. You may answer one or all of the questions below or write your own. The subject of your writing is your choice.

1) Think about your future. How might the information in this chapter help you make better decisions in the future? **2)** Think about your relationships. How might the information in this chapter help you build or heal and repair relationships you find important? **3)** Think about your past; what specific decisions would be different had you known this information as a child? **4)** How might life be different if family and friends were provided this information? **5)** Think about your life in five years. If you practiced the information in this chapter consistently, what results would you experience in your life? **6)** If asked to teach a group of youngsters the contents of this chapter, how would you teach them the information? **7)** Who are you if you are not your past? How can these tools help you be this individual today?

FREE GOGI COURSE

The GOGI My Life Story Certificate Course

To earn an official GOGI Certificate please mail the completed course in 1-2 envelopes to: GOGI, PO Box 88969, Los Angeles, CA 90009.

Within 6-8 weeks, GOGI will mail a certificate to the address you indicate.

The requirements for *" The GOGI My Life Story Certificate Course"* are:

1) **Format** ~ Your project must be handwritten on 8.5 by 11 inch paper (school-size). White paper is best. You must complete 15 full pages. 8 sheets of paper can be used. Remember, write neatly. Volunteers read your work. If we can't read it, you may not get credit. Spanish and other languages are fine. Please start your work about 1 inch from the top and leave 1 inch at the bottom and ½ inch on the sides of each page.

2) **Identification** ~ We open a lot of mail each week. Help us out, please. On the top of the FIRST PAGE please make sure you put <u>ALL</u> of your contact info. Housing, facility, address, city, state, zip are needed. At the top of EVERY PAGE, put your LAST NAME, FIRST NAME, and your ID. This helps us keep your course from getting lost.

3) **Submission** ~ You must mail this course to GOGI. You may put up to 5 pieces of paper in an envelope for the cost of a regular letter stamp. When mailing us two envelopes, please put (1 of 2) and (2 of 2) on the outside of the envelopes. You may also send the entire 8 pieces of paper (15 pages of writing) in one large envelope. The address is below.

4) **Content**

   Pages 1-2 Ages Birth to 5: *What is your birth name, where were you born, who was "family" and who were friends? Siblings? Pets? What are the details you were told about these years?*

Pages 3-4 Ages 6-11: *What are your earliest memories? Where did you attend school? What do you remember about friends or teachers, parents, siblings, other family, or lack thereof? What was the worst thing that happened during this time? What was the best thing that happened?*

Pages 5-6 Ages 12-13: *What were your strengths and personality traits that were emerging at this time? What were your hobbies or things you liked to do? Who were your friends? What was your biggest accomplishment? What were your struggles? Were you happy or sad? Explain your experiences and how they may have impacted your future.*

Pages 7-9 Ages 14-18: *This period of life is often filled with realizations and explorations that define future events. This is also a period of great trials for many youth. What were your trials and how did you deal with these years? What were your strengths? What were your hopes, wishes and desires during this period? What went right and what went wrong? Best of times? Worst of times?*

Pages 10-13 Ages 19-25: *What were the defining moments in your young adulthood? What did you experience that changed the course of things? Were there influential individuals who helped you navigate challenges? Write about those things that impacted your life the most, and your perspective on those events from your wisdom of today.*

Pages 14-15 Ages 26 to now: *If you are a GOGI student, write about your GOGI journey, your favorite GOGI Life Tool and your future goals now that you have the GOGI Life Tools to help you create your life. If you are new to GOGI, write about your life during this period and up to today, highlighting your hopes, dreams, wishes and goals for the future.*

5) <u>**Send all 15 pages to**</u> ~ GOGI My Life Story, PO Box 88969, LA, CA 90009

<u>You should receive your certificate within 6-8 weeks of submission.</u>